Forbidden Passages

Writings Banned in Canada

INTRODUCTIONS BY

PAT CALIFIA

AND

JANINE FULLER

CLEIS
PRESS

Published in the United States by Cleis Press Inc., P.O. Box 8933, Pittsburgh, Pennsylvania 15221, and P.O. Box 14684, San Francisco, California 94114.

Book design and production: Pete Ivey
Cover photograph: David Pickell
Cover model: Colleen Lye

First Edition. Printed in Canada. **For distribution information call (412) 937-1555.**
10 9 8 7 6 5 4 3 2 1

Library of Congress Cataloging-in-Publication Data

Forbidden Passages : writings banned in Canada / introduction by Pat Califia and Janine Fuller.
  p. cm.
  ISBN 1-57344-020-5. — ISBN 1-57344-019-1 (pbk.)
  1. Homosexuality—Literary collections. 2. Gay men—Sexual behavior—Literary collections.
  3. Lesbians—Sexual behavior—Literary collections. 4. Erotic literature, American. 5. Gays' writings, American. 6. Prohibited books—Canada. 7. Censorship—Canada. I. Califia, Pat.
  PS509.H57F67   1995
  810.8'0353—dc20
                                                                    95-33490
                                                                    CIP

"Dead: Carved into Roses" from *Empire of the Senseless* ©1988 by Kathy Acker. Used by permission of Grove/Atlantic, Inc.

"Mama" from *Trash* ©1988 by Dorothy Allison. Used by permission of Firebrand Books, Ithaca, New York.

"Drawing the Line on Censorship" by Diane Anderson from *Deneuve* Vol. 1, #4, Nov/Dec 1991. Reprinted with permission of *Deneuve* magazine. Photos from *Drawing the Line: Lesbian Sexual Politics on the Wall* by Kiss & Tell, Press Gang Publishers, Vancouver, Canada, 1991

"Brother to Brother: Words from the Heart," by Joseph Beam, from *In the Life*, edited by Joseph Beam. Copyright ©1984 Joseph Beam. Used by permission of Alyson Publications, Inc.

"Egg Sex" from *Susie Bright's Sexual Reality* © 1992 by Susie Bright. Used by permission of Cleis Press.

Excerpts from "The Surprise Party" from *Macho Sluts* by Pat Califia. Copyright ©1988 by Pat Califia. Used by permission of Alyson Publications, Inc.

Excerpt from "Numb" from *Frisk* ©1991 by Dennis Cooper. Used by permission of Grove/Atlantic, Inc.

Excerpt from *Hothead Paisan #7* ©1992 by Diane DiMassa and Giant Ass Publishing, P.O. Box 214, New Haven, CT 06502.

Excerpt from *The Man Sitting in the Corridor* ©1991 by Marguerite Duras reprinted by permission of Blue Moon Books, Inc.

Drawings from *Tom of Finland: Retrospective* (1988) reprinted by permission of Tom of Finland Foundation.

"Merit Badges" from *My Biggest O*, edited by Jack Hart. Copyright ©1993 by Jack Hart. Used by permission of Alyson Publications, Inc.

"Eating the Other" from *Black Looks* by bell hooks. Copyright ©1992 by Gloria Watkins. Reprinted with permission from South End Press, 116 St. Botolph St., Boston, MA 02115, (800) 533-8478.

Excerpt from "Gay Studies as Moral Vision" from *Gay Ideas* © 1992 by Richard D. Mohr. Reprinted by permission of Beacon Press.

"Anal Pleasure and the Anal Taboo" from *Anal Pleasure and Health* ©1986 by Jack Morin reprinted by permission of Down There Press, 938 Howard St #101, San Francisco, CA 94103.

"Epilogue: On Writing Pornography," by John Preston, from *I Once Had a Master*. Copyright ©1984 by John Preston. Used by permission of Alyson Publications, Inc.

The portion of *Contract With the World*, "Alma Writing," (Naiad Press, 1982) by Jane Rule is reprinted with the kind permission of the author and the publisher.

"The Daddy Closet" (originally appeared as "Unraveling the Daddy Fantasy") by Marcy Sheiner and "Daddy's Little Girl" by Ann Wertheim are reprinted from *On Our Backs*, Vol. 7, #5, May/ June 1991. Used by permission of *On Our Backs*, 530 Howard St. #400, San Francisco, CA 94110.

"Spiral" from *Memories that Smell Like Gasoline* by David Wojnarowicz (Artspace, 1992). Used by permission of the Estate of David Wojnarowicz.

Contents

A Note from the Publisher

As a press that publishes progressive books by women (and a few men) we rely on courageous, informed, and politically astute booksellers to make "unpopular" culture popular.

So do you.

If you enjoy reading cutting edge erotica, off-center political tracts, small press poetry, or literature catering to refined and unusual interests, know it or not, you depend on courageous booksellers.

Without independent booksellers, grassroots literary culture does not exist. Neighborhood bookstores—gay, feminist, literary, socialist, general—are hothouses of cultural experimentation. When new literary culture emerges, you can bet it was sprouted in the world of alternative publishing.

Like any censor, the Canadian government understands this when it chooses to target shipments of books on their way to Canada's trade bookstores. Little Sister's understands this when it chooses to sue the Canadian government over its customs policies.

So even if the book you are holding in your hands was purchased from a large chain bookstore in the United States, its presence there relies on the continued health of stores like Little Sister's Book and Art Emporium in Vancouver, Canada.

Forbidden Passages: Writings Banned in Canada features excerpts from some of the most significant publications seized at the Canadian border as sexually "degrading," "obscene" or politically suspect. Published as a fundraiser to help Little Sister's pay for more than two hundred thousand dollars in legal costs incurred in their recent litigation against Canada Customs, this book hopefully will raise awareness of censorship both in the U.S. and in Canada.

Not surprisingly, Cleis Press has run into more than a little trouble trying to make available to Canadian readers a book of writings and art already seized in Canada. As of this writing, we are still hopeful that this book can be sold in Canada—where thousands of readers and an activist, loyal bookselling community are waiting for it. Canadian booksellers can order *Forbidden Passages* from Marginal Distribution, 277 George Street N., Unit 102, Peterborough, Ontario K9J3G9. (705) 745-2326.

We have been helped in this project by many, many writers, artists, booksellers, publishers, distributors, attorneys, and anticensorship activists who researched titles, explained arcane Customs procedures, sent us books, scanned text, offered advice and moral support. We would especially like to acknowledge: Pat Califia (who suggested a fundraising anthology for Little Sister's), Lawrence Boyle from L'Androgyne in Montreal, Kimberly Mistysyn from Glad Day in Toronto, Carol Seajay at Feminist Bookstores News, and Anne Griepenburg from Inland Book Company. Inland, perhaps the largest exporter of lesbian and gay literature in the world at the peak of the border seizures, has struggled to keep alternative books available.

Finally, the following publishers supported this project by generously granting permission to use these materials and by waiving permission fees: Alyson Publications, Artspace, Beacon Press, Blue Moon Books, Deneuve, Down There Press, Firebrand Books, Giant Ass Publishing, Grove/Atlantic, Naiad Press, On Our Backs, Press Gang, South End Press, Tom of Finland Foundation.

We hope you find these selections as provocative and informative as we do, and we thank you for supporting Little Sister's with your purchase.

Cleis Press
October 1995

Dangerous Tongues

Forbidden Passages came into being to support the single most important legal challenge which feminists, gay men, lesbians, and anybody who cares about their right to read will face in this century. A royalty on each copy sold will be donated to the defense fund for Little Sister's Book and Art Emporium, a gay bookstore in Vancouver that has challenged the mass seizures of gay and feminist literature at the Canadian border. These seizures have threatened the survival of Canada's four gay bookstores. The finest writers and graphic artists appearing in books and magazines today have had their work confiscated, held up, damaged, and destroyed by Customs agents who are determined to keep radical sex and politics out of their country. The contents of this book give you an idea of the range of material that has become contraband in Canada. This project is also intended to spread the word about the Little Sister's case, because feminist and gay magazines in America have kept a strange sort of silence about it.

Perhaps this silence is motivated by nationalism. It's hard to get Americans to care about struggles for women's rights or queer liberation in other countries. Also, it's quite clear that sexually-explicit material is being targeted for suppression, especially those depicting anal sex, S/M, and other pleasures which in Customs' view are "violent and degrading." Too much of the American women's movement remains under the thumb of antiporn ideology, and too many of the gay literati have let post-AIDS shame about sex numb their First Amendment sensibilities, for me to expect a mass outcry on behalf of the works of John Preston, John Rechy, and myself, among others. But this state of affairs cannot be allowed to continue. What has happened in Canada can happen here, and if it does, our ability to imagine a world free of sex- and gender-based oppression will be injured, perhaps fatally.

It isn't fashionable to talk about censorship. People don't like it. It makes them uncomfortable to be reminded that governments have this power and frequently exercise it. It's frightening to think about books being burned, presses and bookstores being trashed or put out of business, and editors, publishers and authors being sent to jail or fined. *What the state can do to a piece of paper, it can do to the human body.* By limiting what we can read about, the state limits our agenda for social change. When any medium of expression is hampered by police powers, we lose some of our latitude to criticize the institutions that govern our lives. We lose some of our already-puny ability to make these institutions accountable. So we have to be vigilant about censorship. We have to find out when it's happening (no easy task), and we have to oppose it with every ounce of our strength.

That includes the kind of censorship that is practiced by institutions less powerful than the federal government or even a local police chief. I am talking about a bookstore that refuses to carry *On Our Backs, Hothead Paisan, Macho Sluts,* or the *NAMBLA Journal;* a magazine that refuses to print certain articles, images, or advertising; a gallery that removes troublesome pictures of sex, nudity or violence; a performance space that will not host Holly Hughes, Karen Finley, Keith Hennessey, or Ron Athey; even down to the most petty level of the personal disclosures you will not allow your friends to make or the confessions that would make you leave your lover if she ever dared to whisper them in your ear. The intolerance of vice squads, customs agents, and judges has to come from somewhere. It comes from within us, from our intolerant and timid hearts. The source of censorship is our lack of compassion, our fear of difference, our reluctance to see the cracks in our image of The Truth.

We must address our complicity with the censors because they select their targets with an acute sense of our shame, cowardice, ignorance, and discomfort. When the state tries to control what we can read, hear, or see, it does not (at least in the beginning) attack Broadway plays, the daily newspaper that everyone reads on his or her way to work, best-selling novels, or prime-time television. To be at-risk for censorship, a work must meet two criteria. It must say unpalatable things, and it must seem indefensible (either because of the extreme content, or because its maker or distributor lacks the material resources to protest state infringement). Like all bullies, censors are rather cowardly themselves. So they go after things that can't be described on the evening news or reproduced in a newsstand magazine; things that might amuse, shock, or arouse us, but are for that very reason difficult to justify; things that seem expendable and trivial.

We tend to be passive consumers, tourists gawking at the rainbow-colored waterfall of electronic information, pigs slurping at the trough of cable television and Tower Records. We want to see and hear things that entertain us. But we don't want to work too hard for our entertainment, and we don't want to think about how much our responses are individual and how much they are conditioned by multinational corporations that trade in data and images, manipulating the mass consumer libido as ruthlessly as some hospitals in India sell black-market organs for transplant to

Pat Califia

wealthy Westerners. There are so many cable television stations, so many newsgroups on the Internet, it looks as if anything and everything were available. But in fact, it is not. The media that we can access easily are homogenized, sanitized, and banal. We need the forbidden and the unspeakable not only because it has intrinsic worth, but because it reminds us that we exist in a digitized culture where we're taught to crave food that does not nourish us, cookie-cutter relationships, clichés disguised as inspiration, religions without ecstasy, second-hand violence, third-hand sex, two-dimensional lives that are three sizes too small.

If we were not so passive, every one of us would be an artist, an actress, a musician, a writer, a performer, a carpenter, a sculptor, a potter, a revolutionary, a visionary making our unique perceptions visible, audible, and concrete. This loss of our creative potential is one of the least-visible consequences of censorship. We are intimidated by the grand scale of what we see in the mass media, and we never get to see how that stuff is produced. The creative process has been mythologized, and so has the process of finding an audience. I suspect it is also because our hearts have been broken once too often. The stuff that keeps us on the couch for an hour before we fall asleep next to people we don't want to have sex with leaves the bitter after-taste of a carnival con. It takes a rare sort of sociopath to develop the ambition to be the hands inside the waldoes that run this huge game of three-card monte. It is internalized self-censorship which has made it possible for industrial capitalism to create a consumer class.

I don't have any documentation for this. I don't have any statistics to quote or studies to put in a footnote. Either you know what I am talking about, or you don't. Either you get a headache when you watch MTV, or you dance with your coffee table. Either you turn off CNN knowing somebody has been lying to you, or you feel superior and well-informed. Either the radio is your salvation during rush-hour traffic, or you break the knobs when you turn it off because you are so angry about all that three-chord white-boy whining. Some doomed unfortunates believe that it really matters what deodorant they buy, what cereal they eat, who's in the Top Ten, what the super models are wearing, how leading men with big box-office draws are wearing their lapels and their bangs these days. You either see yourself in the cathode-ray tube of what's laughingly called civilization, or you know you are a ghost in the machine, and that invisibility is one of the very few things that might guarantee your safety. The only reason perverts and rebels can exist is because the system is so damned big, they can't find us with their stun guns and debugging programs. We are glitches in the horizontal hold, pixels that are the wrong color, viruses tormenting a harddrive, songs played backwards, piggy-back programs chipping fractions of a cent off the bourgeoisie's ATM deposits.

Pat Califia

People with transgressive sexualities are always hiding, always on the run, even if only in a psychological or emotional sense, because pleasurable sex has always been a reliable target for moral reformers and politicians seeking reelection. I'm not talking about the sublimated kind of sex that's used to sell cars and bottled cappuccino, faux-sex that tries to get you to substitute maxing out your credit card for screwing somebody through the mattress. I'm talking about the kind of material that provokes hard-ons, wet-ons, and ejaculations of both genders: gray market and black market media that say things about the body that a lot of people don't want to hear (even if they secretly agree with it). Pornography is as unpopular with most governments as seditious rhetoric because it has a similar function. Political dissidents voice their discontent with business-as-usual; they say out loud that the emperor has no clothes. Pornography is the grand brawling voice of sexual frustration and panic. It is the only media we have that reliably attacks sex and gender and says, what I have isn't good enough, I don't believe I am the person they say I am, this isn't working, I need something different, I need somebody different, I need more! Pornography is to our injured twentieth-century libidos what medieval churches were to thieves on the run: sanctuary, an unconditional refuge from normalcy and inadequacy, a respite from responsibility, failed relationships, imperfect physiques, and baffled genitalia. Despite its tendency to become commercialized, like everything from food to medicine to air in a capitalistic society, visiting the realm of pornography is a good deal more healthy and a damn sight cheaper than the compulsory annual pilgrimages some people make to Disney World.

Despite the popularity of pornography, it is very difficult to get people angry about anti-smut campaigns. Even in the gay and lesbian community, where we have had to confront at least some of society's sex taboos before we could know ourselves and come out, too many of us remain hostile to sexually-explicit literature and ignorant about its role in the formation of modern gay and lesbian communities. Heterosexual society says we are scum because of our deviant sexuality. Some of us respond to that by embracing eroticism and deviance, by upping the ante of outrageousness, and refusing to be anything other than brazen and defiant in our pleasures. Others respond by rejecting anything that smacks of impropriety or titillation. Like the reformed whore of the proverb, we become fierce supporters of the same anti-sex ideology that outlaws lesbian passion or a man's desire for another man's flesh.

When I see lesbians picketing porn shops, it chills me to the bone. *We are pornographic.* Lesbians are indecent. We offend community standards. We have very little, if any, socially redeeming value because society does not want us, will deny us housing and work and safety on the streets if we let it.

It has never been safe to say out loud, "I am a lesbian," or describe what we do with our hands, tongues, and vulvas to prove our love for other women. The bare fact of our existence has repeatedly been treated as an obscenity. When we collaborate with censorship, we become collaborators in our own oppression. We may not like what other people do with their freedom of sexual speech. But the historical record makes it clear that until that right is secure, lesbians will remain marginalized, shadowy figures just out of range of the world's peripheral vision, as afraid of each other as the New Christian Coalition is of us.

The history of lesbian literature in the West is the history of a few brave women who were willing to be called pornographers if that meant they could speak a little of their truth about being dykes. *The Well of Loneliness* is probably the most famous episode from this history. In 1926, Radclyffe Hall went to her lover, Una Troubridge, and asked for her permission to write a book about lesbians, or, in the terminology of the time, female inverts. She was afraid that publishing such a book would create a scandal that would humiliate her lover and derail her own career. Hall had just enjoyed some commercial success with a book entitled *Adam's Breed,* so she thought she might be able to get a hearing for this controversial and almost literally unspeakable topic. This is what Troubridge told "John," as she called her lover:

Dangerous Tongues

> I am glad to remember that my reply was made without so much
> as an instant's hesitation: I told her to write what was in her heart,
> that so far as any effect upon myself was concerned, I was sick to
> death of ambiguities, and only wished to be known for what I was
> and dwell with her in the palace of truth.[1]

Today, this book has very few fans. The main character, Stephen, is arrogant and self-centered. The author makes no distinction between Stephen's masculinity and her homosexuality. The existence of one deviant trait guarantees the existence of the other. Hall sought to win the sympathy of her readers by having Stephen give up her "normal" female lover, Mary, to Martin, a heterosexual man. Mary leaves Stephen because she is convinced that her lover has cheated on her and does not want her any more. Hall's ignorance about femme dedication to lesbian passion seems wrong-headed today. But we must look at this work in context, as a groundbreaking and daring effort to create lesbian visibility. I find it difficult to imagine how Hall and Troubridge gathered enough courage to come out in the twenties. The consequences of publishing *The Well of Loneliness* were about as dire as John had predicted. The book caused a firestorm of controversy.

In 1928, the book was banned in England at the request of the Home Secretary. But Compton McKenzie's vicious anti-lesbian satire,

Extraordinary Women, was allowed to circulate. George Bernard Shaw and H. G. Wells were among the prominent authors who protested this censorship. Expert witnesses, including Hall, were not allowed to speak at the British trial in defense of her book.

Hall's American publisher, Alfred Knopf, had set type for the book, but withdrew when their attorneys advised them they could be prosecuted. So D. S. Friede of Covici-Friede took up the gauntlet and published an American edition of *The Well of Loneliness* in 1928. The book sold more than twenty thousand copies, which was enough to make it a bestseller for its time. John S. Sumner, secretary of the Society for the Suppression of Vice, complained that the book violated the penal code relating to the circulation of indecent literature. Detectives seized more than eight hundred copies and served a summons on Friede. He and his partner, P. Covici, termed the seizure and court action as "absurd" and vowed to fight it "as far as it can be carried."[2]

Two copies of the book were given to Magistrate Bushel in the West Side Court. On February 22, 1929, *The New York Times* reported that the magistrate had ruled that *The Well of Loneliness* was obscene. Here is an excerpt from Bushel's opinion:

> The book here involved is a novel dealing with the childhood and early womanhood of a female invert. …Her sex experiences are set forth in some detail and also her visits to various resorts frequented by male and female inverts. …To quote the people's brief: "It is a well-written, carefully constructed piece of fiction, and contains no unclean words." Yet the narrative does not veer from its central theme. …The unnatural and depraved relationships portrayed are sought to be idealized and extolled. The characters in the book who indulge in these vices are described in attractive terms, and it is maintained throughout that they be accepted on the same plane as persons normally constituted, and that their perverse and inverted love is as worthy as the affection between normal beings and should be considered just as sacred by society. …The book can have no moral value, since it seeks to justify the right of a pervert to prey upon normal members of a community…it does not argue for repression or moderation of insidious impulses. An idea of the moral tone which the book assumes may be gained from the attitude taken by its principal character towards her mother, pictured as a hard, cruel, and pitiless woman because of the abhorrence she displays to unnatural lust, and to whom…the former says: "But what I will never forgive is your daring to try and make me ashamed of my love. I'm not ashamed of it; there's no shame in me."[3]

What was Magistrate Bushel talking about when he claimed that the "invert" Stephen's "sex experiences are set forth in some detail"? It isn't until page two hundred and eighty-five that Stephen and Mary actually get down to it. Stephen has been in love with Mary for some time, and rather than tell her so, in typical butch fashion, she simply acts like a grouch and ignores her. Mary finally insists that they talk. Stephen finally confesses that she loves Mary, but then feels obligated to give her a long speech about the negative consequences of being her lover.

> ...Mary turned on her with very bright eyes: "You can say that— you, who talk about loving! What do I care for all you've told me? What do I care for the world's opinion? What do I care for anything but you, and you just as you are—as you are, I love you! Do you think I'm crying because of what you've told me? I'm crying because of your dear, scarred face...the misery on it...Can't you understand that all that I am belongs to you, Stephen?"
>
> Stephen bent down and kissed Mary's hands very humbly, for now she could find no words any more...and that night they were not divided.[4] [NB: All ellipses except the first are in the original text.]

Luckily for modern lesbian literature, on April 19, 1929, a three-man appellate court read the opinion of the lower court, read the book, and unanimously came to a contrary opinion. In a very brief decision, they held that *The Well of Loneliness* was not obscene. It continued to be banned in England, however.

The great significance of this case, according to Jonathan Katz, author of *Gay American History*, is that "since the book was allowed open circulation no theme, as a theme, has been banned by our courts."[5] Unfortunately, lesbians who create art about their sexuality now face legal strictures that Katz could not have foreseen in 1976. And it is other women, many of them lesbians and feminists, who have spearheaded this attack. Lesbian desire is still controversial, and the state is still attempting to suppress art and literature about our politics, relationships, and pleasures.

In the 1920s, Radclyffe Hall could not write about lesbians at all without being deemed obscene. Today, I am in a similar position as a leather dyke. I can't write about my people, my life, my lovers, my friends, my chosen family, without being deemed obscene. Authors who write about heterosexual characters frequently gloss over their sexual behavior on the assumption that everybody already knows how that happens, what that looks like. Besides, everybody "knows" that it takes no talent to depict sexual conduct in a literary way. I question both of these assumptions, but I am not particularly interested in writing corrective books about heterosexual passion. I don't have that liberty because there is so much ignorance about and prejudice against sadomasochistic sex. You can't leave sex out of books about the leather community because the rest of you don't know about us. You don't know how we feel about ourselves, our partners, our sex. And often, because of the silence that surrounds aberrant sexuality in this culture, S/M people themselves are afraid to find out what their fantasies would look like if they were ever fulfilled. Am I trying to corrupt and influence susceptible minds? You bet I am.

Last fall, I found myself in a Canadian courtroom, defending my work, which had been seized at the border by Canada Customs. This is one of the most difficult things I have ever done, persuading a bunch of straight, white men that they should not burn my books. I had to go through every section of every book I had ever written and explain, almost page by page, what my intentions were, what I thought the readers' responses would be, and why these ideas should be allowed free circulation. The story "The Surprise Party" in *Macho Sluts* received special attention. Until the last page of this story, the reader has every reason to believe that it is a description of three cops sexually assaulting a lesbian. Then it is revealed that it was in fact a complicated, staged S/M scene produced as a labor of love for the heroine's birthday (hence, the title).

Pat Califia

It would not have surprised me to learn that "The Surprise Party" had provoked the wrath of Canada Customs because it was full of rough sex and bondage, including butt play. But I had forgotten just how twisted sexual politics can be. When liberals become censors, they come up with some novel rationales. "The Surprise Party" was under suspicion for potentially instigating antigay violence. The state was attempting to censor a piece of gay writing under the guise of protecting us from homophobic assaults. At one point, I believe I commented to the court that heterosexual policemen were apparently telling me as a lesbian author that I did not have the right to have sexual fantasies about cops. Nobody laughed. At least I had received a privilege that Radclyffe Hall was never given, the right to appear on the witness stand and speak out on behalf of my own work.

But this is 1995. There's no such thing as censorship anymore, is there? How did this come to be?

In 1992, the Canadian Supreme Court issued a decision in the case of *Regina v. Butler* which radically altered that country's censorship policies. Prior to *Butler*, Canada's definition of obscenity was based on community standards. For instance, *The Body Politic*, Canada's only national gay publication, was put out of business in the early 1980s by repeated prosecutions for obscenity. Charges were brought against *The Body Politic* for publishing feature articles about man/boy love and fist-fucking. *Butler*, ironically, had been brought by civil libertarians who were seeking to overturn such regulation of sexually-explicit media. The court found that free-speech protection does not extend to pornography. Justice John Sopinka wrote the opinion for the court, and he stated, "If true equality between male and female persons is to be achieved, we cannot ignore the threat to equality resulting from exposure to…certain types of violent and degrading material." Canadian censorship had a new justification: protecting the equality of women. And the definition of what types of material were proscribed had assumed much larger proportions.

The language of this decision was based in part on a brief submitted by the Women's Legal Education and Action Fund (LEAF), who had composed their brief with the help of American antiporn feminist Catharine MacKinnon. In 1983, MacKinnon and Andrea Dworkin succeeded in getting Minneapolis to pass a law that defined pornography as a violation of women's civil rights. The law would have allowed any woman who felt that she was harmed by pornography to file a lawsuit against anyone who trafficked in pornography. This bogus civil-rights legislation had a much broader definition of pornography than the current American definition of obscenity. (I should explain that the word "pornography" is not a legal term, and does not appear in American statutes.) Mayor Donald Fraser vetoed this legislation twice. In 1984, Indianapolis also passed this law. Eventually our own Supreme Court found it to be unconstitutional on the grounds that it would restrict speech protected by the First Amendment, it was overbroad and vague, and constituted prior restraint. It took MacKinnon nearly ten years to get Canada to come to the opposite conclusion.

The first successful prosecution after *Butler* was at Glad Day Bookshop. On April 2, 1992, an undercover policewoman walked into the store and asked to see a copy of the lesbian S/M magazine *Bad Attitude*. Clerk Tom Ivason showed her a copy, which she bought. A few weeks later, the policewoman returned and arrested Ivason and the owner of the store, John Scythes. Judge C. H. Paris of the provincial division of the Ontario Court rejected arguments that since there were no men in the magazine, *Butler* did not apply. The judge was especially distressed by Trish Thomas's story, "Wunna My Fantasies," which depicts forceful, but consensual, sex between two women in a shower room. The bookstore was found guilty and given a small fine. Because of the low amount of financial damages, the store felt an appeal would be unsuccessful. LEAF did not offer Glad Day any assistance in fighting this trial. Members of Toronto's Squad P continue to visit Glad Day Bookshop periodically to harass the clerks and owners, and tell them what they have to remove from their shelves.

While censorship in Canada did not begin with *Butler*, this decision acted like a green light to those government officials favoring censorship. When Glad Day sued Canada Customs in 1986 to get them to release *The*

17

Dangerous Tongues

Joy of Gay Sex, which had been seized because it depicted anal sex, a judge ordered Customs to stop such seizures. With the *Butler* decision as fuel, Customs seizures escalated to an alarming degree. Material that featured anal sex could subsequently be seized on the grounds that it was "violent and degrading."

Feminist antiporn laws are not enforced by feminists. They are enforced by straight, homophobic men who think that lesbianism is much more dangerous and degrading to women than domestic violence or rape. Literally thousands of gay and lesbian books have been halted at the border, most of them bound for one of the four gay bookstores in that country. David Leavitt, Dorothy Allison, Susie Bright, Marguerite Duras, John Rechy, Jane Rule, John Preston, and other prominent authors' works have been seized. Safer-sex literature and books about AIDS have been stopped. Even two of Andrea Dworkin's books and the anthology *Against Sadomasochism* have been halted. Madonna's *Sex* was not halted because Time Warner paid their fleet of corporate attorneys to meet with Customs officials and argue that the book had nothing to do with sex, and was merely violent. Bret Easton Ellis' *American Psycho* was also not prohibited. Adult bookstores and X-rated video stores have been untouched by *Butler*. They continue to remain open, selling straight smut.

However, we should not assume that these seizures are an accident, a side-effect of a law that MacKinnon and Dworkin did not foresee. In an interview for a gay newspaper in San Francisco, Dworkin told journalist Tim Kingston:

> The *Butler* decision is probably the best articulation of how pornography, and what kinds of pornography, hurt the civil status and civil rights of women. ...Most obscenity laws are based on a hatred of women's bodies and homophobia: the Canadian law is very different. [*Butler*] includes the concept of harm to women as part of the obscenity standard. ...It says, essentially, that the Canadian community does not accept harm to women as a public standard.[6]

However, when Customs seizures began to receive bad publicity, and a challenge was filed by a gay bookstore, Dworkin changed her tune. She told Jeffrey Toobin, a reporter for *The New Yorker*:

> I was consulted and asked my opinion [by LEAF], and I asked them not to support that obscenity law. This is something MacKinnon and I disagreed on. We agree on a lot of things, but not this one. My position on obscenity law is unequivocal. ...The whole idea of obscenity law is based on the idea that women's bodies are

Pat Califia

18

filthy and shouldn't be displayed, and that homosexuality is disgusting and shouldn't be seen.[7]

MacKinnon told Toobin that "the homophobia reeks" in the Glad Day Bookshop conviction. However, she added, "I am not necessarily at all clear that should not be prosecuted," and said this was not the first time that gay men and lesbians had been "used by pornographers."

Little Sister's is a very small queer bookstore in Vancouver that serves as that city's gay community center. It is about the size of my living room, and has been bombed twice. They sued to stop Customs seizures, claiming that the law was being enforced in a way that discriminated against gay men and lesbians, and further claiming that issues of obscenity are too complicated to be resolved by poorly-trained Customs agents, and should fall within the purview of the courts. The fact that Customs has seized books like *Hot Hotter Hottest*, a chili pepper cookbook, would seem to bolster their argument that Customs agents are less than careful. The case took several months to present, and we are still waiting for a verdict. Whichever way it goes, the decision will probably be appealed. The case has received very little publicity in the United States.

As gay people, we have limited access to our own history. Very few gay men and lesbians (even activists) remember today that the first gay organizations in this country had to fight several running battles with the U.S. Postal Service before they could mail out any literature to their members. In 1925, Henry Gerber was arrested along with two other leaders of the Society for Human Rights, Inc., one of the first homophile organizations to form in this country. One of them was married. His wife had found some of the group's literature and handed it over to Chicago police. A judge decided that it was against federal law to mail "obscene" material like their pamphlet, *Friendship and Freedom*, and bound them over for trial. Charges were eventually dismissed, but Gerber lost his job, and the Society folded.

In the late fifties, the post office invoked a federal obscenity statute against *One, Inc.*, claiming that the organization's magazine was obscene and could not be sent through the mails. In *One, Inc. v. Oleson*, the Court of Appeals of the Ninth Circuit found that the magazine and its contents were obscene. But this ruling was eventually reversed by the Supreme Court in 1958. The year before, the high court had radically revamped and liberalized obscenity laws (at least in regard to the written word) in the *Roth* case. The standard for obscenity under *Roth* was the effect a piece of writing would have on the average man given contemporary community standards. Obscene material was that which appealed to prurient interest. If it weren't for one Samuel Roth, a New Yorker who had previous convictions

Dangerous Tongues

for sending obscenity through the mail, the gay press would never have been able to establish itself in this country.

There is still censorship in the United States. Law enforcement focuses mostly on X-rated videos and, to a lesser extent, on magazines containing photographs of sexual activity. Even the Meese Commission concluded that the written word was beyond the long arm of the law. But it would be a mistake to assume that this protection is ironclad and eternal. In Bellingham, Washington, newsstand owner Ira Stohl and manager Kirstina Kjelsand are being prosecuted for selling *Answer Me!*, a controversial, adults-only magazine that features graphic accounts of rape. Stohl and Kjelsand had refused to remove the magazine from their shelves when ordered to do so by local cops. If convicted, they could spend up to five years in jail and pay ten thousand-dollar fines. The woman who originally complained to the cops about the magazine, Laura Bergstrom, now says she thinks the charges should be dropped, and has told reporters, "The magazine doesn't make people rape. It talks about what caused people to get to that point. It can be used as a positive thing." She also has indicated that she no longer wants to testify against Stohl and Kjelsand, and doesn't want them to go to jail. But District attorney Dave McEachran says he has gotten lots of other complaints about the magazine, and the case will go forward.

Although federal and local law-enforcement cops in America don't go after books, U.S. Customs officials are under no such strictures. They have broad powers to search and seize printed matter coming into this country. In 1992, U.S. Customs officials seized two separate shipments of books and other literature en route to Boston's Glad Day Bookshop. A gay guide to Spain was among the "obscene" material that was confiscated. In 1991, U.S. Customs officials attempted to halt Della Grace's book of lesbian erotic photographs, *Love Bites*. After vigorous protest from Sasha Alyson, the American distributor, the book was finally released. Most of the Customs seizures are made of material going to individuals. Most people are afraid to complain or challenge such an intimidating act. There's no way of knowing just how many (or exactly what kind of) books our own Customs people halt at our borders. But, just as in Canada, U.S. Customs officials seize material that is not obscene and not illegal to produce or distribute within our own borders.

There are other forces as well in our society that want to strictly limit what other people can read. Organizations that monitor attempts to ban books in school and public libraries report that such campaigns are on the upswing and becoming increasingly more successful. For the most part, library book-banning campaigns are waged in an attempt to prevent minors from having access to information about human sexuality, birth control, safer sex, and homosexuality.

The social climate in the United States is pro-censorship. We should

20

Pat Califia

not assume that our First Amendment would prevent laws like *Butler* from being enacted here. The legal theories of Catharine MacKinnon are very popular. If a law school is sophisticated enough to digest the concept of feminist legal theory, MacKinnon's works are on the syllabus. She believes that pornography is not speech, but is instead an act of violence against women, and thus should not be given any First Amendment protection at all. Instead, the broad class of offensive materials which she labels "pornography" should be prosecuted as an act of violence or, at the very least, discrimination. Through sheer repetition, these extremely problematic ideas are gaining broader public acceptance. She is the first source journalists call for a quote on how women feel about pornography. Through bills like the recently-defeated Pornography Victims Compensation Act, she and her allies continue to turn her theories into public policy and law. This vaguely-worded law would have allowed people who had been "victimized" by "pornography" to sue the people who had produced it. Exactly what kind of victimization might occur was not clearly defined in the proposed bill, and once again, the category of materials that MacKinnon calls "pornography" is much broader than the materials that are currently proscribed as obscenity. I am afraid that in another ten years, American obscenity law will look a lot more like Canada's.

21

Dangerous Tongues

As much as Andrea Dworkin and Catharine MacKinnon scare me, I am even more frightened of the people who will enforce their so-called "feminist" antiporn laws. In the wake of the Meese Commission, President Reagan's antiporn task force, the Justice Department has embarked upon a crusade against adult video producers in this country. Racketeer-Influenced Corrupt Organizations (RICO) laws allow them to seize the assets of people accused of breaking the law even before they are convicted of a crime. Multiple prosecutions are often mounted in several different states, which makes a defense prohibitively expensive. Often prosecutors will drop charges in return for the assets of a company and a written promise that the individuals concerned will leave the adult film industry. Relatively few adult videos are being made now, compared to the heyday of the industry in the eighties. The quality and diversity of the product has declined. This hostile climate has made it even more difficult for women to produce their own erotic videos, which we were beginning to do in the mid-eighties. One by one, the recommendations of the Meese Commission are being fulfilled.

Child pornography laws have already created a legal mechanism that could theoretically be used to ban S/M material. On the grounds that this is necessary to protect children, we have federal and state laws which make it a crime to produce, distribute, or possess child pornography. I think we all want to protect children from violence and sexual abuse. But these laws are badly written. In order to qualify as "child pornography," material featuring minors need not be sexually explicit. In fact, Stephen Knox was recently convicted of possessing "child pornography" because he owned some videos that featured children in clothing, who were not engaged in any sexual activity. I can foresee a day when S/M will be thought to be so dangerous to public safety that lawmakers and the courts will uphold regulations against "sexually violent" material, which will be so broadly and vaguely defined that it will include most fetish literature and art.

One of the more frightening things to come down the turnpike is a bill proposed by Senators Jim Exon (D-Nebraska) and Slade Gorton (R-Washington) which would amend the Telecommunications Reform Bill. Bill S-314 would give jail terms and one hundred thousand-dollar fines to anyone who sent private messages that could be lewd, obscene, or harassing on the Internet. In its original form, the bill would have made carriers such as America Online or Delphi responsible for the content of the millions of pieces of e-mail that they transmit every day. Exon says the Communications Decency Act of 1995 is necessary to protect children from sexually-explicit material on the Internet, but the law applies to communication between adults that is as private as a letter or a telephone call. It would obviously have far-reaching effects on a major industry. A petition against the bill, circulated on the Internet, has been signed by more than one hundred thousand people, but it can't be e-mailed to Exon's office, since he is not on-line.

Sexually-explicit material is very popular. People, including women, want to be able to enrich their fantasies, masturbation, and partnered sex with X-rated videos, magazines, photos, CD-ROMS, e-mail, on-line conversation, and books. Why, then, are so few of us willing to defend the people who make this material available? Why do we continue to let censors hold the moral high ground? I think we can do better than this for ourselves. If we want to live in a world free of sexism and homophobia, I believe we must defend all expressions of sexuality. This is not a trivial matter. Sex is the place where we are most whole, it is where our strength and joy comes from, it is the way we bond with one another and make communities. When we defend our sexuality, we are protecting the quality of our lives and even our right to be here, to be visible, to reach out to one another.

By buying this book, you can make a commitment to protecting the right that each of us should have to know about our sexuality, consider the political implications of our pleasures and our beliefs about sex roles and gender, seek out more pleasurable and healthy ways of relating to other people, create art and literature that includes the erotic, and educate our children so they don't have to grow up in an atmosphere of sexual ignorance and fear. Please consider extending that single radical act into a lifetime commitment to free expression. It's so easy to join anti-censorship groups and keep track of the censors in your own city, state, and country.

22

Pat Califia

A single appearance by a calm adult who believes in the First Amendment can make the difference between a library committee banning a book or keeping it on the shelves. A letter to the editor in your daily newspaper can make it clear that there is no consensus about the putative dangers of pornography or the necessity for an expensive campaign to shut down adult bookstores. The staff of bookstores who make a wide range of reading material available will appreciate hearing that you support their decision, and the staff of bookstores who censor controversial material will be very unhappy if you tell them politely that you think their antisex policies are wrong.

Yes, I am asking you to become a sex radical. It's the best sort of radical to be. Because when you get more information about your own sexuality and make it safe for your friends and partners to communicate honestly with you about their sexuality, the quality of your life improves immediately. When you free your body from the invisible control of church and state, you not only challenge some of the most evil authoritarian institutions in the world, you have more fun and better orgasms.

You may not agree with many of the things I've said in this introduction, or some of the positions I take in my work. Perhaps you won't like some of the pieces that appear in *Forbidden Passages*. But don't you think you ought to have the right to read them in the first place? The conversations about sex, gender, violence, and representation that have begun within feminism and the gay movement are vital, and this book is certainly not the last word. But if books can be warehoused and destroyed, we can't even get the raw data we need to be able to disagree intelligently with one another.

If you buy only one gay or feminist book this year, it should be *Forbidden Passages*. Because *Forbidden Passages* represents a vital struggle to keep gay and feminist books in circulation. If we lose this battle because the justice system is homophobic, that will be tragic. But if we lose it because we as a community could not raise enough money to pursue all the legal options of self-defense that are available to us, we should just put our hands in our pockets and quit pretending to care about any kind of social change or progress. Buy this book, hold a benefit, make a donation. Gag the state, before it chokes you!

Pat Califia
August 1995

Notes
1. Katz, Jonathan. *Gay American History: Lesbians and Gay Men in the U.S.A.*
   Thomas Y. Crowell Company, 1976, p. 397.
2. Katz, pp. 398-399.

3. Katz, pp. 402-403.

4. Hall, Radclyffe. *The Well of Loneliness.* Garden City, New York: The Sun Dial Press, 1928, p. 285.

5. Katz, p. 404.

6. Kingston, Tim. "Canada's New Porn Wars: 'Little Sister' Gay/Lesbian Bookstore Battles Canadian Customs," *San Francisco Bay Times*, Nov. 4, 1993.

7. Toobin, Jeffrey. "X-rated," *The New Yorker*, Oct. 3, 1994.

Pat Califia

The Case Against Canada Customs

When a customer asks why Little Sister's Bookstore doesn't have a particular book or magazine, the most frequent response is: Canada Customs. Material that is available all across the United States—from corner stores to major bookstores to local libraries—is often unavailable in Canada due to detentions and seizures by the government. The ambiguities and outright hypocrisies of not only the laws, but the ways in which such laws are enforced, often make it impossible to tell a customer exactly *why* a particular book or magazine might have been held. Why, then, does a country renowned for its innovative social programs and democracy have the most repressive laws at the borders?

Certainly this conundrum comes as no shock to the Canadian gay and lesbian bookselling community who have been fighting the government's legal actions for a decade. After countless appeals, repeals, and redeterminations on Customs seizures and bannings of books and periodicals, we are only too familiar with the enormous power of Customs officials to regulate words and images. Seizing and detaining goods at the border sometimes takes place in the blink of any eye; other determinations are made after some deliberation (fifty or more titles in a day—that's a lot of speed reading!) but leave the importers puzzling over the rhyme and, especially, the reason for the bannings. Without access to either the books or the knowledge of Customs' actions, the public is unaware not only that a book has been banned, but that it even exists at all.

In April of 1986, Glad Day Bookshop in Toronto filed a case against Customs challenging its ban on *The Joy of Gay Sex*. One year later, the case was heard in the Ontario courts. Just blocks away from Glad Day, other booksellers were selling the heterosexual version of the same book, *The Joy of Sex*. In gay and lesbian bookstores and libraries, the demand was there, but the shelves were empty. The similarities of the two books were hard to miss: same publisher, same design, same format. In addition, both featured anal penetration. For gay and lesbian bookstores, this meant the removal and banning of *The Joy of Gay Sex*. Somehow, within a heterosexual context, anal penetration had not been ruled inadmissible, although the obscenity legislation makes no such distinction. The Glad Day case meant to challenge these hypocrisies in Customs guidelines, but the inconsistencies were never addressed in the final ruling. While the judge overturned the original decision by the Deputy Minister's department to ban the book, and ordered it admissible into Canada, the celebrations, unfortunately, were short-lived. Customs detention notices, with the all-too-familiar box marked *Anal Penetration,* continued to arrive at gay and lesbian bookstores notifying them of more and more delays and seizures of various books.

In the spring of 1987, while the Glad Day case was being heard, Little Sister's in Vancouver was arguing for the release of several issues of *The Advocate.* Although the Little Sister's case would eventually be dismissed due to a last minute reversal of the Customs' decision, the shipment of magazines would never be delivered to the store. Ordered by the judge to return the magazines to Little Sister's, Customs was unable to comply as they had destroyed every single copy before the case had even begun. The court awarded the bookstore damages in the amount of the destroyed magazines—a few hundred dollars—nothing close to what it had cost to prepare for the legal case. With an ever-growing list of seized books and banned titles, the bookstore would have to re-organize its strategy in order to combat the relentless detentions of gay and lesbian magazines and books at the border. Appealing books on a case by case basis was not only financially unviable, but would have little effect on future Customs decisions. Bringing a case against Customs itself appeared to be the only logical solution.

The work that appears in this collection represents a cross-section of the kinds of seizures that have occurred throughout the history of Customs Tariff Legislation. Under the current system, the same people who judge the grade of steel, or the percentage of man-made fiber in the weave of a garment, might well be called on to decide the admissability of a book. While the censorship laws have little to do with "literary standards," some Customs agents claim that their decisions are based on "literary" merit; others admit to simply scouring the pages of a book for three infractions, perhaps like tic-tac-toe, to rule the book obscene. Consequently, a large number of decisions appear to be based on coincidence and confusion. The second seizure of *The Mad Man* by famed science fiction writer Samuel Delany took place within weeks of the first, despite assurances that the book would no longer face detentions. Dorothy Allison's *Trash* was identified as a banned book by a computer system set up to track previous decisions of inadmissibility, but the book had never been stopped before. The confusion happened because another book with the same title had been held, and as they had no author's names listed in the computer system, they simply banned the wrong book.

**Janine
Fuller**

Exactly how is the process *supposed* to work? Prepare to be very confused, check all logic at the door, and then you may enter the maze of contradictions that govern Canada Customs decisions. First, imagine that you are a book. You want to go to Canada. There are several points of entry, border crossings, including the post office, and you may stop at more than one of them. At some, you are pulled out of your shipment simply because of your title. *Strokes,* a book on rowing, was considered suspiciously suggestive, and detained. At other crossings, the entire shipment is held and everything is put aside for further examination. This is the introductory level of the detention process: the hunting expedition. The Customs officer, who opens the box and decides to detain the shipment for examination, and the "commodity specialist," who classifies obscenity, deciding whether to ban or release a book, will rule based on the guidelines suggested in the Customs Memorandum D-911.

If you are a book such as Pat Califia's *Macho Sluts*, you have a long history of seizures and detentions at the border. On April 21, 1989, *Macho Sluts* was detained. On July 14, 1989, the book was ruled "prohibited" by a Tariff Value Administrator, at the Section 60 level. On October 24, 1989, on appeal to the highest level of the Customs hierarchy, Section 63, the ruling was overturned by the Deputy Minister in charge of Customs. After a six month wait, and a very rare successful appeal, *Macho Sluts* had been allowed entry into Canada. Gay and lesbian booksellers celebrated the decision; *Macho Sluts*, however, continued to be stopped across Canadian borders despite its admission at the highest level. On May 6, 1992, en route to Little Sister's Bookstore, *Macho Sluts* was prohibited again, three years after its original determination as admissible into Canada. Another six months passed before the book received a ruling at the Section 60 level of appeal. Again and again, Califia's book has been stopped—once, just prior to the Little Sister's trial where she was scheduled to testify. *Macho Sluts* has gone through this process five times now: copies seized while others are already going through the review process, or just after they have been ruled on. Each time *Macho Sluts* is found admissible. The lesson? No decision to release material is binding on future determinations, even at the first level of opening a package at the border. No level is accountable to another, although a book may be detained because it was found earlier to be obscene.

Why would anyone allow rulings on banned books or magazines to stand, without following the appeal process? Quite simply, appealing is a difficult and sometimes daunting task. I've spent hours on the phone with various groups of bureaucrats trying to figure out exactly which forms I should be filing for an appeal, where to get them and how to do it. For individuals receiving their first Customs form, there is a certain amount of intimidation at seeing the words *obscene* and *banned* with your name attached to them. Many people feel intensely invaded by this procedure and worry about the consequences of other people knowing that they had tried to import obscene material into Canada. Ironically, people who have had a magazine or book seized by Customs often need only walk down to a local variety store or visit their nearest bookseller to find the exact same magazine available without any trouble at all.

Although decisions on seizures can be challenged in court, the variety and scope of material being stopped is overwhelming. If the detention of a book can attract public attention, the work often has a much better chance of getting through. Seizures that garner the most public attention are of works by recognizable mainstream authors, while works by emerging and alternative writers and publishers suffer because they do not enjoy the public outcry that a big name can attract. When Marguerite Duras' and Salman Rushdie's works were stopped, all eyes were fixed on Customs.

Janine Fuller

No one, however, knew the power of a name better than Time Warner, the publishers of Madonna's hotly anticipated coffee table book *Sex*. Marketing was Madonna's forte; the advance publicity for her new book was almost unprecedented in the publishing business. With rumors flying about the actual content of the book, Canada Customs braced itself for what would be an onslaught of media and public attention to the book's treatment at Canadian borders. Time Warner, anticipating that the book might have a bumpy ride, prepared their defense and hired one of the most prestigious law firms in Canada to represent them. The book arrived at the Prohibition Importations Directorate in Ottawa for pre-review, under armed guard at the request of the publisher, who was concerned about leaks to the public about the book's contents. During its review at Customs, between August 28, 1992 and October 1, 1992, there were seventeen reports to the Privy Council of the Canadian Government regarding the status of the review. An internal memorandum, drafted in part by Linda Murphy, acting Director of the Prohibited Importation Directorate, revealed that while they were concerned about the contents of Madonna's book, there were stronger fears that its detention would "resurrect and refocus the continuing debate of whether the government should be in the censorship business." Under the ever-watchful public eye, Madonna's book was ruled admissible. No concrete evidence, however, would be made available to the Little Sister's trial lawyers as to why the decision had been made.

The media outcry over the detention of books by Duras, bell hooks, and David Leavitt produced similarly quick releases, although officials were often at a loss to describe their change of heart. David Leavitt's *A Place I've Never Been* was seized on its way to Glad Day Bookshop in

Toronto, just as Leavitt was scheduled to appear at the city's prestigious Harbourfront Writer's Festival at the annual gathering of international authors. When Salman Rushdie's *Satanic Verses* was stopped for review, Canada became the only Western nation to detain the book. An embarrassed Brian Mulroney, then Prime Minister of Canada, issued a terse statement condemning the seizure, although Linda Murphy, under oath, was still unwilling to admit that any mistake had been made by Customs.

In the case of Kathy Acker's *Empire of the Senseless*, the Customs agent assigned to review the initial decision to ban the book took it home for the weekend to evaluate its contents. Public pressure had been mounting with a newspaper account of the seizure. After reading the entire book, the Tariff Value Administrator testified that he could not find any artistic merit to render the book admissible in Canada, until he read the novel's final sentence, which he understood to be a disclaimer of the violence that had occurred throughout the work. The last line was the only redeemable reason for the book's entry into Canada.

The Case
Against
Canada
Customs

One of the most frustrating aspects of these appeals is that the agents' decisions are often absurdly arbitrary and therefore unreliable as general rules. While on the stand, the Customs agent responsible for the initial banning of Duras' *The Man Sitting in the Corridor* still saw no reason why it should have been admissible into Canada. The case of Dennis Cooper's *Frisk* was equally perplexing since the hard-cover edition in question had been sold in the country for the past year and the paperback version had been selling briskly at bookstores throughout Canada. These detentions received a great deal of press, and consequently, their initial bannings were overturned.

A predominate reason for not allowing books into Canada has been their inclusion of any description or depiction of anal sex. Not surprisingly, only weeks before the Little Sister's case was set to begin, "Anal Penetration" was removed from the D-911 memorandum as a basis for banning images and text. Although many people thought this change would stem the tide of detentions, redeterminations began to appear based on grounds that hadn't existed on the original banning forms of certain books. If a book had been banned for its depiction of "Anal Penetration," it would be re-evaluated, and under the changing set of guidelines, reappear inadmissible for different reasons: "Sex with Violence," "Bondage," or the ever-obscure category of "Other." For gay and lesbian bookstores, it was becoming increasingly apparent that simply revoking a category was not going to have the liberating effect we had anticipated. Different rules, same Customs agents.

A number of books, including scholarly works by university presses, have been unjustly suspected and held. The much-anticipated arrival of Richard Mohr's *Gay Ideas* brought an all-too-predictable Customs detention notice, simply because it included some of Robert Mapplethorpe's photographs to illustrate its discussion of current gay controversies. The fact that books like Mohr's, *The Gay and Lesbian Studies Reader* and bell hooks' *Black Looks* have been detained under suspicion of "obscenity" or "hate literature" is alarming. The collection of Latin American short stories, *My Deep Dark Pain Is Love* was stopped on more than one occasion, as was Joseph Beams' *In the Life*, a collection of black gay writing. If hooks' work can be mistaken for hate propaganda, what do they make of these stories of gay existence and sexuality?

Perhaps the detention of Jane Rule's *Contract with the World* can illuminate the senselessness of such outrageous decisions. While under cross-examination, the Customs officer responsible for the initial seizure of Rule's book said that she pulled the novel because she thought it might be hate propaganda: "It just...sounds like it might have a political theme." After reviewing the book and satisfying herself that it did not constitute hate literature, the officer decided that it might be inadmissible based on the sexual nature of the book: it had the word "erotic" on the back cover. Books that offer informative advice on sexual exploration, *Anal Pleasure and Health, The Lesbian Sex Book,* and even *Susie Bright's Sexual Reality,* have been repeatedly detained. Why? Because they are how-to guides to all our sexualities? Because they are empowering?

The supervisor in Rule's case, however, advised the officer that the book should be released immediately without any further review because he recognized Rule as a "fairly mainstream writer." Although he may also have recognized her as an outspoken writer who was one of the government's harshest critics about Customs detentions and legislation, name recognition does not guarantee the admissability of one's work. Writer John Preston also gained recognition in Canada, not just for his outstanding work as an editor of several collections of short stories, but for his work as a writer of erotic fiction. Like Pat Califia, his name would become synonymous with any discussion on censorship, and many of his works continued to be banned in Canada right up to the time of his death. Even death, however, does not protect you from being seized at Canadian borders. Oscar Wilde's *Teleny* was stopped on more than one occasion and a biography of Noel Coward was held in the summer of 1994. Since 1986, *Erotic Poems from the Greek Anthology* has remained a banned book.

Books produced and marketed in Canada also find difficulty at the border. Gayle Baudino's science fiction novel, *Shroud Of Shadow,* didn't even have to cross a border; it was somehow rerouted through the postal system and ended up detained and reviewed by Customs, within Canada. Complete with a Penguin of Canada sticker on the box, and a Canadian postal stamp, the package arrived at Little Sister's marked *Cleared by*

Janine
Fuller

Customs. The art collective Kiss and Tell had photographs from *Drawing the Line,* a show touring in the U.S. stopped at the border and held, while ironically, *Deneuve,* a lesbian magazine that had reviewed the show and included pictures of the exhibition, was stopped for its portrayal of bondage, and was never delivered to its destination: Little Sister's bookstore in Vancouver, the hometown of the artists.

While David Wojnarowicz's *Memories That Smell Like Gasoline,* his intensely personal visual diary, was stopped en route to Little Sister's, and was eventually released, other artists haven't fared as well in their attempts to enter the country. Tom of Finland's works have hardly ever made it across the border, except for the odd calendar or biography. Perhaps it's all those orgies with uniformed guards that so disturb the Customs officers. Comic books like *Hothead Paisan # 7*—the adventures of a lesbian terrorist and her cat—have been stopped at the border as well for their portrayal of "sexual degradation." Since that particular issue had openly pro-choice content, it's far more likely that the "political" message was the offending one.

Such detentions at the border have brought groups like PEN International and booksellers' associations from around the world out in full force to publicly condemn Canada Customs operations. Some of the people who signed such declarations, Sarah Schulman, Dorothy Allison, and David Leavitt among them, found their own books on the ever-growing list of Customs detentions.

Little Sister's and B.C. Civil Liberties Association began their latest court challenge against the Canadian government in 1990. This time, we were no longer novices, and we were no longer relying on the integrity of the system to change unfair legislation simply by ruling on one detained book or magazine. We arrived with a different kind of court challenge, one that would shake the very existence of Customs authority and its censorship powers. For the first time, the history of Customs seizures and detentions would be under attack, and so would the legislation governing them. The suit was a two-fold challenge: first, to Customs' right to detain material before it is deemed obscene, by charging that prior restraint of material is unconstitutional under section 2{b} of the Canadian Charter of Rights and Freedoms; and second, to the way Customs has administered its powers by unfairly discriminating against gay and lesbian authors, readers, distributors and publishers, under Section 15 of the Charter, the right to equality under the law.

The trial date was to begin in the fall of 1991, but it was delayed, rescheduled, and postponed in an attempt by the Crown lawyers representing Customs to dismiss the case. The motion was denied but the case would wait another year, scheduled for the fall of 1993. Again, only weeks prior to the beginning of the trial, the government's lawyers requested a motion to adjourn the case on the basis that there was not enough court time allotted for the case to be heard. Again, despite great opposition from the Little Sister's council, the trial was delayed.

In addition to the time and money that had gone into preparing for the trial that year, and in light of the previous delays, there were also some very real concerns about the health of some of the Little Sister's witnesses. In particular, one of most important witnesses, author John Preston, had been living with AIDS, and his health and ability to testify were in question with each passing day. After preparing one of the most thoughtful submissions to the trial, on his life and work, Preston died the spring before the case was finally heard. Other witnesses would also not live long enough to be heard in the courts, such as Jay Scott, one of Canada's most respected film critics, and Customs Broker David Goble, a long-time associate of the bookstore.

Janine Fuller

On October 4, 1994, the case that had begun as a simple one-week trial, costing a few thousand dollars, had finally started. Only now, after years of delays, the case would be heard for forty days, at an astounding price tag of two hundred and fifty thousand dollars. Although the endless delays had created a tremendous amount of media coverage both nationally and internationally, the witnesses who appeared in the case garnered the most attention. Respected writers, academics and activists from both sides of the border spoke out to testify for Little Sister's. While owners of feminist and comic book stores expressed their surprise at their recent problems with Customs, booksellers from gay and lesbian bookstores gave vivid histories of the endless Customs detentions they had experienced throughout the last decade. The testimonies ranged from predictable detentions due to sexual content to the unimaginable seizures of magazines like *Deneuve* and the *New York Native*, novels by Marcel Proust, biographies on Cole Porter and Michelangelo; even the vegetarianism of *The Sexual Politics of Meat*, the anti-pornography espousal of *Against Sadomasochism* and the work of Andrea Dworkin were elicited as evidence of the injustice of Customs rulings.

While stories of banned books filled the courts, so, too, did their defense. Writers like Jane Rule and Sarah Schulman defended both the works of other banned authors, like Pat Califia and John Preston, as well as their own works of fiction that had been stopped at the border. One of the most anticipated witnesses, Pat Califia, had the daunting task of explaining in detail the process she went through as a writer and an S/M activist when writing books like *Doc and Fluff* and *Macho Sluts*. She defended her work in a way that only Pat Califia could: unflinchingly. Nino Ricci, past winner of the Governor General's Award for Fiction, and Pierre Berton, one of the most prolific authors in Canada, were also called to testify. Sociologists, anthropologists and psychologists took the witness stand as well. Carole Vance, renowned for her essay collection *Pleasure and Danger,* described how pornography has evolved to reflect the changing attitudes of the society it represents. Throughout the trial, the absurdities and inconsistencies of the system were laid out for all to see. At times, I found myself sitting on my hands to resist clapping after the testimony; at other moments, there were tears from one pew to the next.

None of this could have happened had it not been for the tremendous support, both financial and moral, from across North America. As challenges to censorship in Canada are rarely afforded a victory without court appeals, we must continue to build and prepare for tomorrow's struggles. A rising wave of conservatism on both sides of the border means the victories we've won as gays and lesbians will surely be tested. With two more court levels to pursue, the bookstore and anti-censorship proponents must be as vigilant and determined as ever. Little Sister's is determined to see the case through all the way to the Supreme Court of Canada if necessary. This will take more time and more money, in addition to the debt still owed from the trial in the fall. The government has an inexhaustible supply of taxpayers' money to continue this case. Having been represented by five lawyers, three federally and two provincially, they clearly have little concern with respect to the financial viability of the case. When we've been fundraising for years out of tin cans and glass bottles, books like the one you are about to read are a rare, joyous gift. With the enormous generosity of the writers, artists and publishers involved in the compilation of *Forbidden Passages,* we are building the means to secure a free and democratic society in which everyone has access to ideas, and in which writers and artists can work without fear.

Janine Fuller
August 1995

**The Case
Against
Canada
Customs**

FORBIDDEN PASSAGES

Alma Writing
from *Contract with the World*

JANE RULE

My thirty-first birthday. Did I ever once, in the ten years I lived with Mike, tell him I wanted to write? I've never told anyone. Yet he gave me this absurdly pretentious blank book, which has been sitting on my night table now for three months, growing more pretentious and blanker each day. If it had been a house plant, it would have been dead of neglect in a couple of weeks. The only way to kill this book is to fill it with failed hope. Do I always begin things already knowing they won't work? Like school? Like Mike? Like Roxanne? Like this? If I were going to write something *real,* I'd have to make it up. Scribbling in this reminds me of Vic filling pages with what writing looked like to him because Tony was really learning how. So I read *Sita* and think, enviously, "Anyone can do that," and set out to show myself up because, even if I did know enough about language, my life, unlike Kate Millett's, is only life-sized.

If my chief excuse for living were writing it down, would I live very differently? I'd have to. The moment I got out of bed this morning, I'd have to start packing my bags because I wouldn't be having dinner with my parents and sisters and sons—what a crowd that sounds and is—I'd be going off to Roxanne instead to celebrate my real birth. But even if I did that, I'm far too amazed by loving her to be able to write it down. And anyway, when I get up, I'm going to put on the yellow pantsuit Mother gave me yesterday, my yearly birthday suit, which remakes me into a daughter, and live through the day here in my parents' house, where no one will suggest—perhaps because they don't even think it—that I am an embarrassment or a burden, failed wife, apprehensive mother, with no idea what to do with myself or my children because the one thing I want to do is impossible even if I had the money to do it. And I can't leave this house until I'm sure I won't do it.

When I asked Carlotta all those months ago, right after Mike left, if she'd ever made love with a woman, she said, "Other than myself? No." I let that shut me up. It needn't have. Even when Carlotta didn't want to listen to me, she would, then anyway. I suppose I've been half in love with *her* all these years, and I felt—feel—as guilty about Carlotta as I do about Mike. In a way, Roxanne didn't have anything to do with Mike, or Mike and me, except as a way of showing us how bad it really was.

Is that true? I am so guilty in every direction that I can't understand anything.

I suggested to Dad that maybe I ought to see a psychiatrist. He didn't say no; he wouldn't. He simply said, "Why don't you give yourself some time to think things over for yourself? Then, if you still feel it might help, of course." I've spent most of my time trying not to think things over. I haven't the faintest idea what I'd ask a psychiatrist if I saw one....

Why did I marry? Why did I marry Mike? Aside from the fact that he asked me. Probably aside from the fact that he still, even strained and thin, is the handsomest man I have ever seen, and initially that made me feel that I must be attractive myself, not just a great oversized cow of a girl. Surely not aside from the fact that I thought he was an artist, which made me imagine sensitive depths beyond the repetitive pigheaded nonsense which I thought was simply the surface of his mind. Yes, aside from that, too. Those are my excuses.

Because when I was an eighteen-year-old virgin who had never been on a real date except when it was arranged by my parents, my friend Bett, who had already been "ecstatically" married for two years, taught me the facts of life. She told me I was too tall and too womanly (read: one of monstrous tits) to attract boys and too dumb to attract men. She said "shy." I had to get in touch with my own body, and she could show me how if I could just pretend, while she was doing it, that she was a man. It took her three weeks to get my clothes off, another week to get her hand between my legs, and I never did imagine it was anything but her hand. I was so wet I thought I was hemorrhaging, and I was terrified by what I felt, as if I were being raped not by her hand, but by my own body, which had set fire to itself in some Dickensian spontaneous combustion.

"Am I bleeding to death?"

"That's sex, sweetie."

When I refused to play her part, which she wanted me to do just in order to see that I understood how it worked, she lost interest in the enterprise. Since I couldn't even think about her without beginning to shake, we found it easy enough to avoid each other. Someone told me the other day that she's just married for the third time.

I'm not so worried about what a psychiatrist might make of that as I

Jane Rule

am of the fact that it didn't occur to me until a year ago today that Bett had been attracted to me or I to her. I let myself believe for all those years that I allowed that long, ridiculous seduction in the interest of nothing but self-knowledge. In a sense, because I certainly wasn't in love with Bett, I was right, except, of course, that I didn't want to know. I was so afraid of being betrayed by my own body that feeling nothing but mild discomfort with Mike was a relief. When I realized that at his inaccurate touch I wouldn't begin to melt down my own thighs and burn to my tits, I stopped fighting him off and let him do pretty much what he liked or needed to do as long as it didn't involve me in any active or important way.

One of Mike's arguments for getting married was that women like sex better after marriage, as if the ring had an ancient erotic power. I was nearly sure by then that it didn't. He'd been fucking me on a mattress in the back of his truck twice a week for six months before he tested his theory on a wife in a proper bed in a bridal suite at the Bayshore Inn. I used Vaseline then. I wanted to please him. It wasn't until after Tony was born…What is this myth about forgetting birth? If that kind of terrible commotion could go on, juices spurting out everywhere for an audience of people, of strangers, and afterwards I felt a smug exhibitionist, my breasts full of milk, why on earth was I frightened or ashamed of the wet animality of my own pleasure? I used to want Mike to fuck me just after I'd nursed Tony or even, if he could have been gentle about it, while I was. He was embarrassed even to see me nursing, and when a spot of milk seeped out onto my blouse, I had to change at once. I felt almost innocent in my indignation, married to this prudish ape of a man, a sexual illiterate in an age of information overkill. I even pretended to myself that he was perfectly satisfied. He got it up; he got it in; he got it off. And he was on his way to getting the army of children his vanity required, who, in fact, irritated him to violence for the first three years of their lives and were too expensive for him to support after that.

Why did I marry? Why did I marry Mike? To put off for good knowing that I did not attract men because they didn't attract me. I don't need a psychiatrist to tell me that the only kind of man who insists on marrying a lesbian is a man like Mike, for whom even fucking a brick wall is a test of his virility. Oh, there's the other extreme, a man who wants to pass no tests at all. A man like that could not have protected me from myself for so many hard, safe years.

I was safe. Mike did protect me, and he would have gone on even without the children he still wanted, and I would have gone on, yes, even after Roxanne (she might even have made it easier), if I hadn't finally really seen his pain, not hanging there in the shed but on Joseph's face, in Joseph's simple, humiliating words, "He's unhappy."

Alma
Writing

I don't know how Joseph's wife feels about his going crazy. Maybe she isn't responsible and so doesn't feel betrayed. But if Mike had actually had to kill himself to get away from me, he would have killed me, too. I would have died of exposure. I still have nightmares about the truck smashed up in a pile of cars or going over a cliff, and almost always Mike in miniature is hanging there on the rearview mirror, where he had a nude doll when I first met him.

I couldn't possibly want to get even. In public measure I'm probably way ahead, as long as Mike doesn't contest the divorce. Dad didn't want me to accept the last check, but I told him that would rile Mike, and I don't want Mike angry, even as far away as Arizona. He could so easily, if he wanted to, take the children away from me, have me declared unfit as a mother.

Jane Rule

I don't see Roxanne more than once a week. She knows, because of the divorce, I have to be very careful, and even once that's over, we can't possibly live together, not while I have the boys. But at least we'll be able to have an occasional weekend together. I can always leave the kids here. Roxanne doesn't ask for anything. I'm the one who gets hysterical about not being able to see her. I'm the one who suggests crazy escapes, even without the boys. She shakes that great flower of hair against my belly and says no into my navel.

I love her thinness. I love the tiny cups of her breasts, the way she shows them off in tank tops and see-through shirts. I love her low-slung trousers, so beautifully indecent when she leans over; her cleavage, she says, inviting my finger down to tease the pucker of her ass hole. I touch her wherever and whenever I like. She's as greedy as a cat.

And now I'm trying to be Violette Leduc, writing with one hand, masturbating with the other, and I don't think it's disgusting, but it is stupidly, stupidly lonely to lie here in bed on my birthday, my cunt weeping with greed, while Mother indulges me by cooking breakfast for the children. This should have happened to me when I was fifteen. Is conscience always perverse? I had enough sexual shame for a nun at fifteen, but I had no trouble lying in bed any morning while the bacon cooked. Now, with no sexual shame at all, the smell of this morning's bacon makes both hands equally guilty.

Get up, woman. You're thirty-one years old today, even if you are lying in bed in a room that still suffers traces of your childhood. In twenty minutes Vic and Tony will have to be driven across town to school, and Mother may or may not refrain from saying, "If they transferred schools, they could walk." I can't really tell her the truth: that I don't transfer them because once a week, on Roxanne's day off, I can go to her from dropping the boys without having to explain anything to anyone.

Merit Badges
from *My Biggest O*

JACK HART

When I was thirteen years old, my best friend Tim and I were in the Boy Scouts. We had grown up together, and we were always doing things together. We went on Scout jamborees that lasted a week or two, and we'd camp out, two boys to a tent.

On one of these jamborees, we were hiking together in the woods when we came across a stack of trash. As we looked more carefully, we saw that it was a stack of magazines. There were some *Playboys*, and other magazines, but the one that really attracted our attention was a thick gay porno magazine. It was very graphic, and showed a lot of different sexual positions. We were shocked as we looked through it, because we hadn't known that a lot of these things went on. We did our best to clean up the mess, but Tim took the magazine with him. Later that night, in our tent, Tim pulled out the magazine. Under the dim light of the Coleman lantern, we looked through the magazine and talked about it. Tim asked if I'd ever had sex with anyone. "No," I answered. Had he? No, he said.

We kept on looking at the pictures. Tim said this all looked like fun, and I agreed. We decided to try it.

So we completely unzipped both sleeping bags, and used one for a mattress and the other for a cover, then we took off all our clothes. Tim, like me, was fully aroused. We dimmed the lantern even more, and continued to look at the magazine for guidance.

"What do you want to do?" Tim asked.

I told him we should try everything. We turned off the lantern, and Tim (who I suspect had more experience than he admitted) rolled close to me and we kissed, then caressed each other. It was heaven to me. He kissed me down my chest and belly, then sucked my dick. In what seemed like just seconds I was shooting off. Then I did the same for him.

We rested awhile and looked at the magazine again, then tried intercourse. This time he took off first, using a little spit for lubricant. At first it hurt something awful, but my body just relaxed and it began to feel great. Here I was with my best friend, a person I loved as if he were my own brother, and he was fucking me. It seemed so natural. Then it was my turn, and again it was wonderful.

Naturally that added a different twist to our relationship. We became even closer, and continued having sex for a very long time. Even later, when we both dated and had sex with girls, we still spent nights together in each other's houses, had sex while on walks in the woods, and so on.

At that time, safe sex was not an issue. We loved each other, and sex made that love even stronger. This stands out in my mind as the best sex I ever had because it was unconditional. It was not given for any ulterior motives, and it brought us ever closer.

Tim was my best friend and we did everything together. I visit his memory every Memorial Day. He died in my arms, in Vietnam, in 1968. I love you, Tim...and I miss you very much.

Jack Hart

Drawing the Line on Censorship from *Deneuve*

DIANE ANDERSON

In 1987, the Vancouver lesbian and gay magazine *Angles* came under fire from its readership for printing Li Yuen's poster depicting lesbian sex in celebration of International Lesbian Week. Gay bar owners dumped issues of the magazine in the trash and pulled out all advertising, while some lesbians in the community labeled the imagery pornographic and began a large-scale boycott of the magazine.

This repeat collusion of anti-pornography and feminism—much like the so-called sex debates of the seventies—brought together groups of women to discuss the issues of sexuality and censorship. From one feminist artists' support group sprang the three-woman collective called Kiss and Tell.

The collective, which includes photographer Susan Stewart and models Persimmon and Lizard Jones, has created an audience-participatory, lesbian sex photography exhibit: *Drawing the Line.* One of the most user-friendly art shows around, *Drawing the Line* includes one hundred black-and-white images of lesbian sexuality ranging from passionate kissing to a bathroom shower scene to sadomasochist role play on black satin sheets to sex with a dildo in an underground garage. The images are arranged progressively from "least controversial" to "most controversial."

While the photos have been called "important interventions into feminist debates," the most important facet of this exhibit is the nature of the display. Women viewing the photos are asked to write their comments on the walls around them—recording their reactions to a certain image when they feel it. (Men are asked not to draw or write on the wall—in respect of women's space—but to record their reactions in a comment book.)

"One of the reasons we decided to do our show with the writing on the

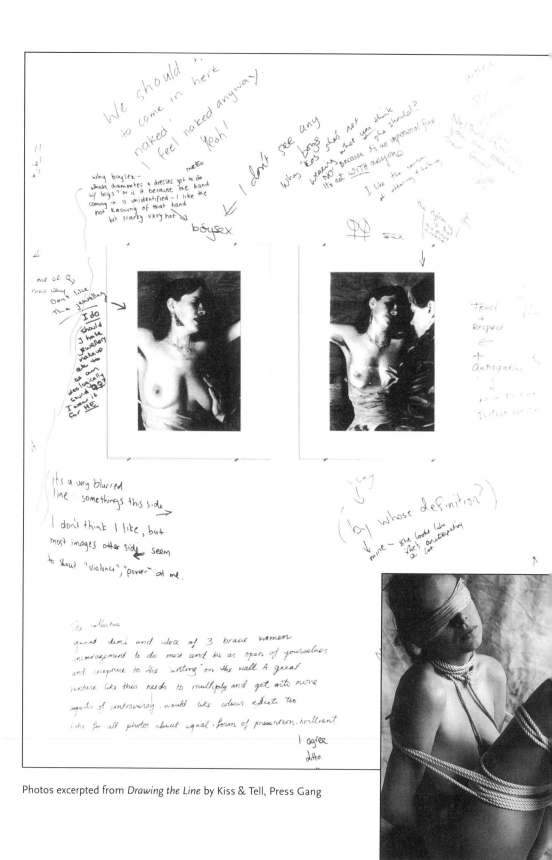

Photos excerpted from *Drawing the Line* by Kiss & Tell, Press Gang

wall and everything was because in the feminist press—in the gay press too—there was this thing called the sex debates," said Jones in an interview in *Rites* magazine. "And it was being framed as an S/M or an anti-S/M debate or a butch/femme or anti-butch/femme debate or a sex radical or anti-sex radical debate. And you were either on one side or the other side.

"It sort of felt like you had to have a position before you even got to react to any of the images or any of the practices," she added. "You had to have a position. And they are fairly complicated positions, and they are kind of difficult positions to have. So we thought we'll just put the pictures up and we'll see how many women react to pictures when they don't feel like they have to have a position and they don't have to be one of the people who writes in the feminist press."

What has resulted at every gallery showing from San Francisco's Camerawork in 1990 to Vancouver to Melbourne and Sydney, Australia to Atlanta, is an often painful, always controversial discussion in the lesbian and feminist communities about sexual imagery, censorship and morality. At every show, women are forced to decide where they "draw the line" on censorship and erotic art.

Because she expected lesbians in San Francisco to have the most tolerant attitudes, Stewart said she was very surprised by the women's reactions.

"We found them to be very mean in San Francisco. There were a lot of nasty comments. One woman would write something and another would write 'Shut up, bitch' in response," said Stewart.

In Australia, women were "furious" with the one image that showed a man watching the two women from the background. Yet, when *Drawing the Line* was on display in Toronto, the same sequence elicited a much different response: "Women were writing things like, 'He's been in my fantasies, too.'"

What was most at issue in the comments? A Toronto reviewer said the issue was love.

"Was there any love in the images? What does it mean to have sex without love? What would a photo of love look like?" said Mary Louise Adams of *Rites* magazine. One woman wrote in four-inch high letters under the very first and most "loving" group of photos (Persimmon and Lizard making out by a waterfall), "SEX WITHOUT LOVE EQUALS ABUSE," Adams noted. Another woman wrote alongside the same group, near a photo of the two women kissing, "This is about love and I love it."

Related to this concern about love was a preoccupation with what's "natural." "Women seemed to be searching for an elusive, essential, unencumbered lesbian sexuality," Adams said. "Love, it seems, is high on the natural, while props, jewelry, and even clothes are not."

While lesbians in big cities like San Francisco debate sexual imagery, women in smaller communities have yet to see the exhibit. As censorship is an ongoing contentious issue in many communities, individual galleries have made quite a statement simply by mounting the show.

"Questions of censorship are particularly burning ones for us as producers," said Stewart. "I can't stand exploitation, but I'm not anti-imagery. I would go to the anti-porn slide shows and get turned on by their pictures. *Drawing the Line* became part of a process of trying to make sense of all this."

The pictures—to some erotic, to some offensive—don't answer any questions, they merely call for a closer inspection, an analysis of sorts.

At a time when censorship issues are on many women's minds, *Drawing the Line* is particularly important because it asks viewers to make choices and form opinions about sexual imagery—lesbian sexual imagery—that could have an effect on even the dominant culture audience.

The response to *Drawing the Line* is a prime example that curbing a form of visual expression doesn't mean it will not be present in society. Whether or not lesbian sexuality is represented, it will always exist. Bringing images like fist-fucking and dildo play to the gallery wall will not thrust those ideas onto us as lesbians, it will merely bring them into the light so they can be discussed with free inquiry.

Diane Anderson

from *The Man Sitting in the Corridor*

MARGUERITE DURAS

The woman went for a walk along the ridge overlooking the river, then came back to where she is now, lying facing the corridor, in the sun. But she can't see the man. She's cut off from the shade inside the house by the blinding glare of summer.

Impossible to tell whether her eyes are half-open or shut. She looks as if she's resting. The sun's already very strong. She's wearing a light-colored dress, made of light-colored silk, with a revealing tear in front. Under the silk the body was naked. It might be a white dress, perhaps. Washed-out, old.

*   *   *

I see that her legs, up till now left lying in a seemingly careless sprawl—I see she's drawing them together now, joining them more and more violently in a deliberate, labored movement. She clamps them together so close, her body's distorted and gradually shrinks to take up less than its usual space. Then suddenly the effort ceases, together with all other motion. Her body lies stretched out straight as a last image. Her head has fallen on to her arm. She's frozen in the attitude of sleep. And looking at her is the man, silent.

*   *   *

She might start to move again. She'd be slow to do so with him looking at her. Knowing that the blue of his eyes, drinking up the light in the dark corridor, is riveted on her. I see she's raising her legs now and separating them from the rest of her body. She does it in the same way as she brought them together, deliberately and with difficulty, and so violently that her body, in contrast to just now, is bereft of its length and distorted to the point of possible ugliness. She freezes again in this position, open to him. Her head's still averted from her body and lying on her arm. She stays like that, in that obscene, bestial position. She's grown ugly. She's become what she'd have been if she were ugly. She is ugly. And she lies there, today, in all her ugliness.

I can see the promontory of her sex between the parted lips, and all the body clenched around it in a heat burning ever stronger. I can't see her face. I can see beauty hovering uncertainly around her face, but I can't make it merge with and belong to it. All I can see is the averted oval and its clear tense side. I think the closed eyes must be green. But I stop at the eyes. And even if I manage to keep them in my own for any length of time, they don't give me the whole of the face. It remains unknown. But I can see the body. I can see it all, violently near. It's streaming with sweat, in a terrifying white blaze of sun.

The man would go on waiting.

And then she'd get there. The sun's so strong she cries out trying to bear it. Bites the arm of the dress where it's already torn, and cries out. Calls out a name. Tells someone to come.

We—she and I—hear footsteps. Hear that he's moved. That he's emerged from the corridor. I see and tell her, tell her he's coming. That he's moved, emerged from the corridor. That at first he moved jerkily, as if he'd forgotten how to walk, and then slowly, very very slowly. That he's coming. That he's here. That I can see the blue of his eyes looking past her to the river.

Marguerite Duras

48

Mama
from *Trash*

DOROTHY ALLISON

Above her left ankle my mother has an odd star-shaped scar. It blossoms like a violet above the arch, a purple pucker riding the muscle. When she was a little girl in South Carolina they still bled people in sickness, and they bled her there. I thought she was just telling a story, when she first told me, teasing me or covering up some embarrassing accident she didn't want me to know about. But my aunt supported her.

"It's a miracle she's alive, girl. She was such a sickly child, still a child when she had you, and then there was the way you were born."

"How's that?"

"Assbackward," Aunt Alma was proud to be the first to tell me, and it showed in the excitement in her voice. "Your mama was unconscious for three days after you were born. She'd been fast asleep in the back of your Uncle Lucius's car when they hit that Pontiac right outside the airbase. Your mama went right through the windshield and bounced off the other car. When she woke up three days later, you were already out and named, and all she had was a little scar on her forehead to show what had happened. It was a miracle like they talk about in Bible school, and I know there's something your mama's meant to do because of it."

"Oh yeah," Mama shrugged when I asked her about it. "An't no doubt I'm meant for greater things—bigger biscuits, thicker gravy. What else could God want for someone like me, huh?" She pulled her mouth so tight I could see her teeth pushing her upper lip, but then she looked into my face and let her air out slowly.

"Your aunt is always laying things to God's hand that he wouldn't have interest in doing anyway. What's true is that there was a car accident and you got named before I could say much about it. Ask your aunt why you're named after her, why don't you?"

On my stepfather's birthday I always think of my mother. She sits with her coffee and cigarettes, watches the sun come up before she must leave for work. My mama lives with my stepfather still, though she spent most of my childhood swearing that as soon as she had us up and grown, she'd leave him flat. Instead, we left, my sister and I, and on my stepfather's birthday we neither send presents nor visit. The thing we do—as my sister has told me and as I have told her—is think about Mama. At any moment of the day we know what she will be doing, where she will be, and what she will probably be talking about. We know, not only because her days are as set and predictable as the schedule by which she does the laundry, we know in our bodies. Our mother's body is with us in its details. She is recreated in each of us, strength of bone and the skin curling over the thick flesh the women of our family have always worn.

Dorothy Allison

When I visit Mama, I always look first to her hands and feet to reassure myself. The skin of her hands is transparent—large-veined, wrinkled and bruised—while her feet are soft with the lotions I rubbed into them every other night of my childhood. That was a special thing between my mother and me, the way she'd give herself the care of my hands, lying across the daybed, telling me stories of what she'd served down at the truckstop, who had complained and who tipped specially well, and most important, who had said what and what she'd said back. I would sit at her feet, laughing and nodding and stroking away the tightness in her muscles, watching the way her mouth would pull taut while under her pale eyelids the pulse of her eyes moved like kittens behind a blanket. Sometimes my love for her would choke me, and I would ache to have her open her eyes and see me there, to see how much I loved her. But mostly I kept my eyes on her skin, the fine traceries of the veins and the knotted cords of ligaments, seeing where she was not beautiful and hiding how scared it made me to see her close up, looking so fragile, and too often, so old.

When my mama was twenty-five she already had an old woman's hands, and I feared them. I did not know then what it was that scared me so. I've come to understand since that it was the thought of her growing old, of her dying and leaving me alone. I feared those brown spots, those wrinkles and cracks that lined her wrists, ankles, and the soft shadowed sides of her eyes. I was too young to imagine my own death with anything but an adolescent's high romantic enjoyment; I pretended often enough that I was dying of a wasting disease that would give lots of time for my aunts, uncles, and stepfather to mourn me. But the idea that anything could touch my mother, that anything would dare to hurt her was impossible to bear, and I woke up screaming the one night I dreamed of her death—a dream in which I tried bodily to climb to the throne of a Baptist god and demand her return to me. I thought of my mama like a mountain or a cave, a force of nature, a woman who had saved her own life and mine, and would surely save us both over and over again. The wrinkles in her hands made me think of earthquakes and the lines under her eyes hummed of tidal waves in the night. If she was fragile, if she was human, then so was I, and anything might happen. If she was not the backbone of creation itself, then fear would overtake me. I could not allow that, would not. My child's solution was to try to cure my mother of wrinkles in the hope of saving her from death itself.

Once, when I was about eight and there was no Jergens lotion to be had, I spooned some mayonnaise out to use instead. Mama leaned forward, sniffed, lay back and laughed into her hand.

"If that worked," she told me, still grinning, "I wouldn't have dried up to begin with—all the mayonnaise I've eaten in my life."

"All the mayonnaise you've spread—like the butter of your smile, out there for everybody," my stepfather grumbled. He wanted his evening glass of tea, wanted his feet put up, and maybe his neck rubbed. At a look from Mama, I'd run one errand after another until he was settled with nothing left to complain about. Then I'd go back to Mama. But by that time we'd have to start on dinner, and I wouldn't have any more quiet time with her till a day or two later when I'd rub her feet again.

Mama

I never hated my stepfather half as much for the beatings he gave me as for those stolen moments when I could have been holding Mama's feet in my hands. Pulled away from Mama's side to run get him a pillow or change the television channel and forced to stand and wait until he was sure there was nothing else he wanted me to do, I entertained myself with visions of his sudden death. Motorcycle outlaws would come to the door, mistaking him for a Drug Enforcement Officer, and blow his head off with a sawed-off shotgun just like the one my Uncle Bo kept under the front seat in his truck. The lawn mower would explode, cutting him into scattered separate pieces the emergency squad would have to collect in plastic bags. Standing and waiting for his orders while staring at the thin black hairs on his balding head, I would imagine his scalp seen through blood-stained plastic, and smile wide and happy while I thought out how I would tell that one to my sister in our dark room at night, when she would whisper back to me her own version of our private morality play.

When my stepfather beat me I did not think, did not imagine stories of either escape or revenge. When my stepfather beat me I pulled so deeply into myself I lived only in my eyes, my eyes that watched the shower sweat on the bathroom walls, the pipes under the sink, my blood on the porcelain toilet seat, and the buckle of his belt as it moved through the air. My ears were disconnected so I could understand nothing—neither his shouts, my own hoarse shameful strangled pleas, nor my mother's screams from the other side of the door he locked. I would not come back to myself until the beating was ended and the door was opened and I saw my mother's face, her hands shaking as she reached for me. Even then, I would not be able to understand what she was yelling at him, or he was yelling at both of us. Mama would take me into the bedroom and wash my face with a cold rag, wipe my legs and, using the same lotion I had rubbed into her feet, try to soothe my pain. Only when she had stopped crying would my hearing come back, and I would lie still and listen to her voice saying my name— soft and tender, like her hand on my back. There were no stories in my head then, no hatred, only an enormous gratitude to be lying still with her hand on me and, for once, the door locked against him.

Dorothy Allison

Push it down. Don't show it. Don't tell anyone what is really going on. We are not safe, I learned from my mama. There are people in the world who are, but they are not us. Don't show your stuff to anyone. Tell no one that your stepfather beats you. The things that would happen are too terrible to name.

Mama quit working honkytonks to try the mill as soon as she could after her marriage. But a year in the mill was all she could take; the dust in the air got to her too fast. After that there was no choice but to find work in a diner. The tips made all the difference, though she could have made more money if she'd stayed with the honkytonks or managed a slot as a cocktail waitress. There was always more money serving people beer and wine, more still in hard liquor, but she'd have had to go outside Greenville County to do that. Neither she nor her new husband could imagine going that far.

The diner was a good choice anyway, one of the few respectable ones down-town, a place where men took their families on Sunday afternoon. The work left her tired, but not sick to death like the mill, and she liked the people she met there, the tips and the conversation.

"You got a way about you," the manager told her.

"Oh yeah, I'm known for my ways," she laughed, and no one would have known she didn't mean it. Truckers or judges, they all liked my mama. And when they weren't slipping quarters in her pocket, they were bringing her things, souvenirs or friendship cards, once or twice a ring. Mama smiled, joked, slapped ass, and firmly passed back anything that looked like a down pay-ment on something she didn't want to sell. She started taking me to work with her when I was still too short to see over the counter, letting me sit up there to watch her some, and tucking me away in the car when I got cold or sleepy.

"That's my girl," she'd brag. "Four years old and reads the funny papers to me every Sunday morning. She's something, an't she?"

"Something," the men would nod, mostly not even looking at me, but agreeing with anything just to win Mama's smile. I'd watch them closely, the wallets they pulled out of their back pockets, the rough patches on their forearms and scratches on their chins. Poor men, they didn't have much more than we did, but they could buy my mama's time with a cup of coffee and a nickel slipped under the saucer. I hated them, each and every one.

My stepfather was a truck driver—a little man with a big rig and a bigger rage. He kept losing jobs when he lost his temper. Somebody would say something, some joke, some little thing, and my little stepfather would pick up something half again his weight and try to murder whoever had dared to say that thing. "Don't make him angry," people always said about him. "Don't make him angry," my mama was always saying to us.

Mama

I tried not to make him angry. I ran his errands. I listened to him talk, standing still on one leg and then the other, keeping my face empty, impartial. He always wanted me to wait on him. When we heard him yell, my sister's face would break like a pool of water struck with a handful of stones. Her glance would fly to mine. I would stare at her, hate her, hate myself. She would stare at me, hate me, hate herself. After a moment, I would sigh— five, six, seven, eight years old, sighing like an old lady—tell her to stay there, get up and go to him. Go to stand still for him, his hands, his big hands on his little body. I would imagine those hands cut off by marauders sweeping down on great black horses, swords like lightning bolts in the hands of armored women who wouldn't even know my name but would kill him anyway. Imagine boils and blisters and wasting diseases; sudden overturned cars and spreading gasoline. Imagine vengeance. Imagine justice. What is the difference anyway when both are only stories in your head? In the everyday reality you stand still. I stood still. Bent over. Laid down.

"Yes, Daddy." "No, Daddy." "I'm sorry, Daddy." "Don't do that, Daddy." "Please, Daddy."

Push it down. Don't show it. Don't tell anyone what is really going on. We are not safe. There are people in the world who are, but they are not us. Don't show your fear to anyone. The things that would happen are too terrible to name.

Sometimes I wake in the middle of the night to the call of my name shouted in my mama's voice, rising from silence like an echo caught in the folds of my brain. It is her hard voice I hear, not the soft one she used when she held me tight, the hard voice she used on bill collectors and process servers. Sometimes her laugh comes too, that sad laugh, thin and foreshadowing a cough, with her angry laugh following. I hate that laugh, hate the sound of it in the night following on my name like shame. When I hear myself laugh like that, I always start to curse, to echo what I know was the stronger force in my mama's life.

As I grew up my teachers warned me to clean up my language, and my lovers became impatient with the things I said. Sugar and honey, my teachers reminded me when I sprinkled my sentences with the vinegar of my mama's rage—as if I was supposed to want to draw flies. And, "Oh honey," my girlfriends would whisper, "do you have to talk that way?" I did, I did indeed. I smiled them my mama's smile and played for them my mama's words while they tightened up and pulled back, seeing me for someone they had not imagined before. They didn't shout, they hissed; and even when they got angry, their language never quite rose up out of them the way my mama's rage would fly.

54

Dorothy Allison

"Must you? Must you?" they begged me. And then, "For God's sake!"
"Sweet Jesus!" I'd shout back but they didn't know enough to laugh.
"Must you? Must you?"
Hiss, hiss.
"For God's sake, do you have to end everything with *ass?* An anal obsession, that's what you've got, a goddamn anal obsession!"
"I do, I do," I told them, "and you don't even know how to say *goddamn.* A woman who says *goddamn* as soft as you do isn't worth the price of a meal of shit!"

Coarse, crude, rude words, and ruder gestures—Mama knew them all. You *assfucker, get out of my yard,* to the cop who came to take the furniture. *Shit-sucking bastard!* to the man who put his hand under her skirt. *Jesus shit a brick,* every day of her life. Though she slapped me when I used them, my mama taught me the power of nasty words. Say *goddamn.* Say anything but begin it with *Jesus* and end it with *shit.* Add that laugh, the one that disguises your broken heart. Oh, never show your broken heart! Make them think you don't have one instead.
"If people are going to kick you, don't just lie there. Shout back at them."
"Yes, Mama."

Language then, and tone, and cadence. Make me mad, and I'll curse you to the seventh generation in my mama's voice. But you have to work to get me mad. I measure my anger against my mama's rages and her insistence that most people aren't even worth your time. "We are another people. Our like isn't seen on the earth that often," my mama told me, and I knew what she meant. I know the value of the hard asses of this world. And I am my mama's daughter—tougher than kudzu, meaner than all the ass-kicking, bad-assed, cold-assed, saggy-assed fuckers I have ever known. But it's true that sometimes I talk that way just to remember my mother, the survivor, the endurer, but the one who could not always keep quiet about it.

We are just like her, my sister and I. That March when my sister called, I thought for a moment it was my mama's voice. The accent was right, and the language—the slow drag of matter-of-fact words and thoughts, but the beaten-down quality wasn't Mama, couldn't have been. For a moment I felt as if my hands were gripping old and tender flesh, the skin gone thin from age and wear, my granny's hands, perhaps, on the day she had stared out at her grandsons and laughed lightly, insisting I take a good look at them. "See, see how the blood thins out." She spit to the side and clamped a hand down on my shoulder. I turned and looked at her hand, that hand as strong as heavy cord rolled back on itself, my bare shoulder under her hand and the muscles there rising like bubbles in cold milk. I had felt thick and strong beside her, thick and strong and sure of myself in a way I have not felt since. That March when my sister called I felt old; my hands felt wiry and worn, and my blood seemed hot and thin as it rushed through my veins.

Mama

My sister's voice sounded hollow; her words vibrated over the phone as if they had iron edges. My tongue locked to my teeth, and I tasted the fear I thought I had put far behind me.

"They're doing everything they can—surgery again this morning and chemotherapy and radiation. He's a doctor, so he knows, but Jesus...."

"Jesus shit."

"Yeah."

Mama woke up alone with her rage, her grief. "Just what I'd always expected," she told me later. "You think you know what's going on, what to expect. You relax a minute and that's when it happens. Life turns around and kicks you in the butt."

Lying there, she knew they had finally gotten her, the *they* that had been dogging her all her life, waiting for the chance to rob her of all her tomorrows. Now they had her, her body pinned down under bandages and tubes and sheets that felt like molten lead. She had not really believed it possible. She tried to pull her hands up to her neck, but she couldn't move her arms. "I was so mad I wanted to kick holes in the sheets, but there wasn't no use in that." When my stepfather came in to sit and whistle his sobs beside the bed, she took long breaths and held her face tight and still. She became all eyes, watching everything from a place far off inside herself.

"Never want what you cannot have," she'd always told me. It was her rule for survival, and she grabbed hold of it again. She turned her head away from what she could not change and started adjusting herself to her new status. She was going to have to figure out how to sew herself up one of those breast forms so she could wear a bra. "Damn things probably cost a fortune," she told me when I came to sit beside her. I nodded slowly. I didn't let her see how afraid I was, or how uncertain, or even how angry. I showed her my pride in her courage and my faith in her strength. But underneath I wanted her to be angry, too. "I'll make do," she whispered, showing me nothing, and I just nodded.

"Everything's going to be all right," I told her.

"Everything's going to be all right," she told me. The pretense was sometimes the only thing we had to give each other.

When it's your mama and it's an accomplished fact, you can't talk politics into her bleeding. You can't quote from last month's article about how a partial mastectomy is just as effective. You can't talk about patriarchy or class or confrontation strategies. I made jokes on the telephone, wrote letters full of healthy recipes and vitamin therapies. I pretended for her sake and my own that nothing was going to happen, that cancer is an everyday occurrence (and it is) and death is not part of the scenario.

Push it down. Don't show it. Don't tell anybody what is really going on. My mama makes do when the whole world cries out for things to stop, to fall apart, just once for all of us to let our anger show. My mama clamps her teeth, laughs her bitter laugh, and does whatever she thinks she has to do with no help, thank you, from people who only want to see her wanting something she can't have anyway.

Five, ten, twenty years—my mama has had cancer for twenty years. "That doctor, the one in Tampa in '71, the one told me I was gonna die, that sucker choked himself on a turkey bone. People that said what a sad thing it was—me having cancer, and surely meant to die—hell, those people been run over by pickups and dropped down dead with one thing and another, while me, I just go on. It's something, an't it?"

It's something. Piece by piece, my mother is being stolen from me. After the hysterectomy, the first mastectomy, another five years later, her teeth that were easier to give up than to keep, the little toes that calcified from too many years working waitress in bad shoes, hair and fingernails that drop off after every bout of chemotherapy, my mama is less and less the mountain, more and more the cave—the empty place from which things have been removed.

"With what they've taken off me, off Granny, and your Aunt Grace—shit, you could almost make another person."

A woman, a garbage creation, an assembly of parts. When I drink I see her rising like bats out of deep caverns, a gossamer woman—all black

56

Dorothy Allison

edges, with a chrome uterus and molded glass fingers, plastic wire rib cage and red unblinking eyes. My mama, my grandmother, my aunts, my sister and me—every part of us that can be taken has been.

"Flesh and blood needs flesh and blood," my mama sang for me once, and laughing added, "but we don't need as much of it as we used to, huh?"

When Mama talked, I listened. I believed it was the truth she was telling me. I watched her face as much as I listened to her words. She had a way of dropping her head and covering her bad teeth with her palm. I'd say, "Don't do that." And she'd laugh at how serious I was. When she laughed with me, that shadow, so grey under her eyes, lightened, and I felt for a moment—powerful, important, never so important as when I could make her laugh.

Mama

I wanted to grow up to do the poor-kid-done-good thing, the Elvis Presley/Ritchie Valens movie, to buy my mama her own house, put a key in her hand and say, "It's yours—from here to there and everything in between, these walls, that door, that gate, these locks. You don't ever have to let anyone in that you don't want. You can lay in the sun if you want to or walk out naked in the moonlight if you take the mood. And if you want to go into town to mess around, we can go do it together."

I did not want to be my mother's lover; I wanted more than that. I wanted to rescue her the way we had both wanted her to rescue me. *Do not want what you cannot have,* she told me. But I was not as good as she was. I wanted that dream. I've never stopped wanting it.

The day I left home my stepfather disappeared. I scoured him out of my life, exorcising every movement or phrase in which I recognized his touch. All he left behind was a voice on a telephone line, a voice that sometimes answered when I called home. But Mama grew into my body like an extra layer of warm protective fat, closing me around. My muscles hug my bones in just the way hers do, and when I turn my face, I have that same bulldog angry glare I was always ashamed to see on her. But my legs are strong, and I do not stoop the way she does; I did not work waitress for thirty years, and my first lover taught me the importance of buying good shoes. I've got Mama's habit of dropping my head, her quick angers, and that same belly-gutted scar she was so careful to hide. But nothing marks me so much her daughter as my hands—the way they are aging, the veins coming up through skin already thin. I tell myself they are beautiful as they recreate my mama's flesh in mine.

My lovers laugh at me and say, "Every tenth word with you is *mama.* Mama said. Mama used to say. My mama didn't raise no fool."

I widen my mouth around my drawl and show my mama's lost teeth in my smile.

Watching my mama I learned some lessons too well. Never show that you care, Mama taught me, and never want something you cannot have. Never give anyone the satisfaction of denying you something you need, and for that, what you have to do is learn to need nothing. Starve the wanting part of you. In time I understood my mama to be a kind of Zen Baptist—rooting desire out of her own heart as ruthlessly as any mountaintop ascetic. The lessons Mama taught me, like the lessons of Buddha, were not a matter of degree but of despair. My mama's philosophy was bitter and thin. She didn't give a damn if she was ever born again, she just didn't want to be born again poor and wanting.

Dorothy Allison

I am my mama's daughter, her shadow on the earth, the blood thinned down a little so that I am not as powerful as she, as immune to want and desire. I am not a mountain or a cave, a force of nature or a power on the earth, but I have her talent for not seeing what I cannot stand to face. I make sure that I do not want what I do not think I can have, and I keep clearly in mind what it is I cannot have. I roll in the night all the stories I never told her, cannot tell her still—her voice in my brain echoing love and despair and grief and rage. When, in the night, she hears me call her name, it is not really me she hears, it is the me I constructed for her—the one who does not need her too much, the one whose heart is not too tender, whose insides are iron and silver, whose dreams are cold ice and slate—who needs nothing, nothing. I keep in mind the image of a closed door, Mama weeping on the other side. She could not rescue me. I cannot rescue her. Sometimes I cannot even reach across the wall that separates us.

On my stepfather's birthday I make coffee and bake bread pudding with bourbon sauce. I invite friends over, tell outrageous stories, and use horrible words. I scratch my scars and hug my lover, thinking about Mama twelve states away. My accent comes back and my weight settles down lower, until the ache in my spine is steady and hot. I remember Mama sitting at the kitchen table in the early morning, stars in her eyes, lying to me and my sister, promising us that the time would come when she would leave him— that as soon as we were older, as soon as there was a little more money put by and things were a little easier—she would go.

I think about her sitting there now, waiting for him to wake up and want his coffee, for the day to start moving around her, things to get so busy she won't have to think. Sometimes, I hate my mama. Sometimes, I hate myself. I see myself in her, and her in me. I see us too clearly sometimes, all the little betrayals that cannot be forgotten or changed.

When Mama calls, I wait a little before speaking.

"Mama," I say, "I knew you would call."

Spiral
from *Memories That Smell Like Gasoline*

DAVID WOJNAROWICZ

1

Back near the monitor the blazing light of the hand jerking the hardened dick is creating a blind spot to the right of it in the room and I can just about make out some silhouetted shape of a guy in shorts and shirt opened, knowing this because as he moves from dick to dick his shirt floats like a curtain billowing into light and disappearing again and he's got a baseball cap on. I'm moving into this blind spot to watch and he's on his knees sucking some kid's prick. There's an old man in the darkest shadows his flesh is a bland color just a dead white, emptied of blood and he seems afraid of the light keeps shifting weight from one foot to the other in a squatting position at some point the sucking guy has his back to the old man and he's leaning over the ledge to get another guy's prick in his mouth and the old man takes a large hand and peels the guy's shorts down in a slow motion insistence and soon has his tongue planted firmly between the guy's cheeks. The guy starts rolling his ass in the air in circular motions and continues sucking the prick of the stranger before him. The old guy is lapping away like a puppy with a bowl of milk and I'm standing there in the darkness and there's a stream of water or something snaking across the floor and the pale glow of faces staring towards us at the monitor that I can only see sideways and on the angled screen is a pair of eyes looking dreamily up at the owner of a fat dick that's slowly sinking down his throat. A man enters the basement and walks over in my general direction momentarily blinded by the monitor and he runs into me before his eyes adjust, instead of backing up he reaches out and pulls me into a hug his arms muscled and hard and his embrace is squeezing air from my lungs. I rub

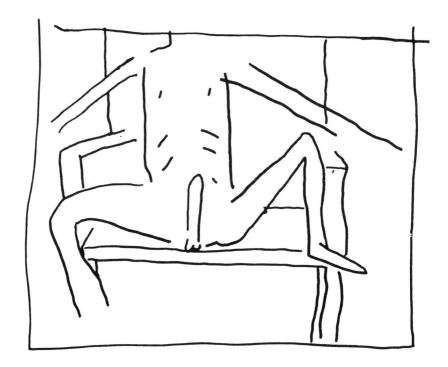

**David
Wojnarowicz**

when I was 9 or 10 some guy picked me up
in central park + took me home. He made
a polaroid of me sitting in a chair. It
didn't show my face so I let him keep it.

my hands over the surface of his body his clothes and an almost indis-
cernible dampness to his shirt his body hard as wood his lips grazing my
neck his hand pulling my head down so that he can softly bite the nape of
my neck dragging his tongue around to my ear up and down the lines of
my throat and my fingers are loosening his belt and my hands slip through
his open zipper into all that warmth inside his underwear and down under
his balls and his hand is on the back of my neck on my shoulders and he's
pushing and I'm sinking down slow into a crouching position and from
there slipping my hands beneath the edge of his white t-shirt and the t-
shirt is tight and he's beginning to sweat his body generating intense heat
and my mouth is opening and I'm licking under his balls the length and
head of his dick is falling across the bridge of my nose resting against my
eyelids and one of my hands swings up to wipe across my mouth to collect
spit and then falls to my cock and I'm slicking it up with spit creating a
random rhythm while licking at the base of his dick his hands are in my

This guy took me home and at one point grabbed my arm and said make a fist. He suddenly pushed it against his butt. My hand disappeared. I was all shook up. Where did my hand go? I wondered.

hair moving around cradling the base of my skull. As I stand back up I'm losing myself in the pale cool color of his flesh in the shadows and he takes my head in his hands and pulls my face close to his gaze and I realize he's one of those guys that you know absolutely that if you'd met him twenty years earlier you both could have gone straight to heaven but now mortality has finally marked his face. He was really sexy though; he was like a vast swimming pool I wanted to dive right into.

2

All I can remember was the beautiful view and my overwhelming urge to puke. I was visiting my friend in the hospital and realizing he was lucky. Even though he was possibly going blind he did get the only bed in the room that had a window and a view. Sixteen floors up overlooking the

David
Wojnarowicz

I was ten years old. An old
guy and his son picked me up and took
me to a motel in midtown. He
demanded that I give him my
underwear to examine. What you
lookin for I asked.   Green spots.
V.D. he said.

southern skies as all the world spins into late evening. It was a beautiful
distance to drift in but I still wanted to throw up. There among the red
and yellow clouds drifting behind the silhouettes of the skyline was the
overwhelming smell of human shit. It was the guy in the next bed; all
afternoon he'd been making honking sounds like a suffocating goose. He
was about ninety years old and I only got a glimpse of him and saw that
they'd strapped an oxygen mask over his leathered face and when he
screamed it sounded like a voice you'd hear over a contraption made of two
tin cans and a piece of wire. Calling long distance trying to get the operator. Someone in charge. Someone in authority. Someone who could make
it all stop with a pill, a knife, a needle, a word, a kiss, a smack, an embrace.
Someone to step in and erase the sliding world of fact.

In this dream there was this young guy about 21 and he was aware that I wanted to kiss him and he demanded to fight. I found I had somehow learned all these great boxing moves - I beat him up just a little to get him to stop bothering me. I still wanted to kiss him.

3

This kid walks into my sleep he's maybe seventeen years old stretches out on a table says he's not feeling well. He may be naked or else wearing no shirt his hands behind his head. I can see a swollen lump pushing under the skin of his arm pit. I place my hands on his stomach and chest and try to explain to him that he needs to be looked at by a doctor. In the shadows of this room in the cool blue light the kid, a very beautiful boy, looks sad and shocked and closes his eyes like he doesn't want to know or like somehow he can shut it all out.

Later some guy appears in the place. He has an odd look about his face. He tries to make it known that he knows me or someone close to me.

David
Wojnarowicz

I was about 10 years old this guy took me to
a hotel on 34 St and 8th avenue and sat in
a chair with out his pants and asked me to
blow him. he promised he wouldn't come in
my mouth. I started sucking him and
his face got red and he came in my mouth.
I remember the wind in the curtains over the bed. I
remember I wanted to kick his ass too.

He leans in close has flat dull eyes like blue silvery coins behind his irises. I
think it is the face of death. I get agitated and disturbed and want to be left
alone with the kid. Try to steer him away to some other location. He disap-
pears for a moment and then reappears in the distance but far away isn't
far enough. I turn and look at the kid on the table he looks about ten years
old and water is pouring from his face.

4

Two blocks south there is a twenty story building with at least three hundred visible windows behind which are three hundred tiny blue television screens operating simultaneously. Most of them are tuned to the same stations you can watch the patterns of fluctuating light pop out like in codes. Must be the war news. Twenty seconds of slow motion video frames broadcasting old glory drifting by in the bony hands of white zombies, and half the population ship their children out on the next tanker or jet to kill and be killed. My friend on the bed never watches his tv. It hangs anchored to the wall above his bed extended over his face and on the end of a gray robotic-looking arm. If he bothered to watch the tv he would see large groups of kids in the saudi desert yakking about how they were going to march straight through to baghdad, find a telephone booth and call home to mom and dad. Then he'd see them writing out their wills on the customary government-supplied short forms. Or maybe he'd catch the video where the commanding instructor holds up a land mine the size of a frisbee and says, If you step on one of these there won't be nothing left of you to find…just red spray in the air. Or the fort dix drill sergeant out of view of the rolling cameras, When ya see those towel-heads…

But my friend is too weak to turn the channels on other people's deaths. There is also the question of dementia, an overload of the virus's activity in his brain short-circuiting the essentials and causing his brain to atrophy so that he ends up pissing into the telephone. He sees a visitor's face impaled with dozens of steel nails or crawling with flies and gets mildly concerned. Seeing dick cheney looming up on the television screen with that weird lust in his eyes and bits of brain matter in the cracks of his teeth might accidentally be diagnosed as dementia. I catch myself just as all this stomach acid floods up into my throat, run out to the hallway to the water fountain.

5

It's a dark and wet concrete bunker, a basement that runs under the building from front to back. There is one other concrete staircase that is sealed off at the top by a street grate and you can hear the feet of pedestrians and spare parts of conversations floating down into the gloom. At a mid-point in the room you can do a 360 degree slow turn and see everything; the shaky alcoves built of cheap plywood, a long waist-high cement ledge where twenty-three guys could sit shoulder to shoulder if forced to, the darkened ledge in the back half hidden by pipes and architectural supports,

David Wojnarowicz

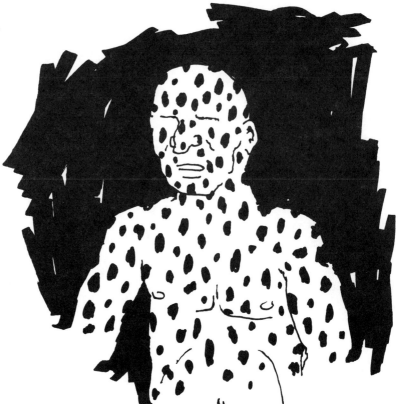

He burst into my home naked and covered in Kaposi threw me on the bed: "you would've thought I was sexy if you saw me before I got sick." I kissed him then pushed him off and ran from the apartment. woke up.

and the giant television set. It's one of the latest inventions from japan, the largest video monitor available and it is hooked into the wall, then further encased in a large sheet of plexiglas in order to prevent the hands of some bored queen from fucking with the dials and switching the sex scenes to Let's Make A Deal. The plexi is covered in scratches and hand prints and smudges and discolored streaks of body fluids. At the moment the images fed from a vhs machine upstairs are a bit on the blink. When the original film was transferred it was jumping the sprockets of the projector and now I'm watching images that fluctuate strobically up and down but only by a single centimeter. Each body or object or vista or close-up of eye, tongue,

I was living in this cheap water
front hotel. A young rich guy lived
down the hall. He would always stay
out late looking for hustlers on the
waterfront. Late one night he appeared at
my door covered in blood: "I made a
mistake I think."

stiff dick and asshole is doubled and vibrating. Kind of pretty and psyche-
delic and no one is watching it anyway. There is a clump of three guys
entwined on the long ledge. One of them is lying down leaning on one
elbow with his head cradled in another guy's hand. The second guy is
feeding the first guy his dick while a third guy is crouching down behind
him pulling open the cheeks of his ass and licking his finger and poking at
its bull's-eye. The shadows cast by their bodies cancel out the details necessary for making the vision interesting or decipherable beyond the basics.
One of the guys, the one who looks like he's praying at an altar, turns and
opens his mouth wide and gestures towards it. He nods at me but I turn

away. He wouldn't understand. Too bad he can't see the virus in me, maybe it would rearrange something in him. It certainly did in me. When I found out I felt this abstract sensation, something like pulling off your skin and turning it inside out and then rearranging it so that when you pull it back on it feels like what it felt like before, only it isn't and only you know it. It's something almost imperceptible. I mean the first minute after being diagnosed you are forever separated from what you had come to view as your life or living, the world outside the eyes. The calendar tracings of biographical continuity get kind of screwed up. It's like watching a movie suddenly and abruptly going in reverse a thousand miles a minute, like the entire landscape and horizon is pulling away from you in reverse in order to spell out a psychic separation. Like I said, he wouldn't understand and besides his hunger is giant. I once came to this place fresh from visiting a friend in the hospital who was within a day or two of death and you wouldn't know there was an epidemic. At least forty people exploring every possible invention of sexual gesture and not a condom in sight. I had an idea that I would make a three minute super-8 film of my dying friend's face with all its lesions and sightlessness and then take a super-8 projector and hook it up with copper cables to a car battery slung in a bag over my shoulder and walk back in here and project the film onto the dark walls above their heads. I didn't want to ruin their evening, just wanted maybe to keep their temporary worlds from narrowing down too far.

6

The old guy is still honking away when I get back to the room. There are tiny colored lights wobbling through the red threads of dusk and I'm trying to concentrate on them in order to avoid bending over suddenly and emptying out. I've been trying to fight the urge to throw up for the last two weeks. At first I thought it was food poisoning but slowly realized it was civilization. Everything is stirring this feeling inside me, signs of physical distress, the evening news, all the flags in the streets and the zombie population going about its daily routines. I just want to puke it all out like an intense projectile. I sidetrack myself by concentrating on the little lights at dusk; imagining one of them developing a puff of smoke in its engines and plummeting to the earth among the canyon streets. Any event would help. The nurse finally shows up and behind the curtains I hear the sounds of a body thumping, the sounds of cloth being rolled up, of water splashing and the covers being unfurled and tucked. Finally she leaves taking the smell of shit with her in a laundry cart. My friend wakes up and starts weeping; he's hallucinating that he can't find something that probably

I saw this in a park on 2nd avenue one night. I wish my eyes were movie cameras so I could record scenes like this in movement.

never existed. I understand the feeling just like I understand it when he sometimes screams that he hates healthy people. A senate group was in new york city recently collecting information on the extent of the epidemic and were told that in the next year and a half there will be thirty-three thousand homeless people with AIDS living in the streets and gutters of the city. A couple of people representing the policy of the city government assured the senators that these people were dying so fast from lack of health care that they were making room for the others coming up from behind; so there would be no visible increase of dying homeless on the streets. Oh I feel so sick. I feel like a human bomb tick tick tick.

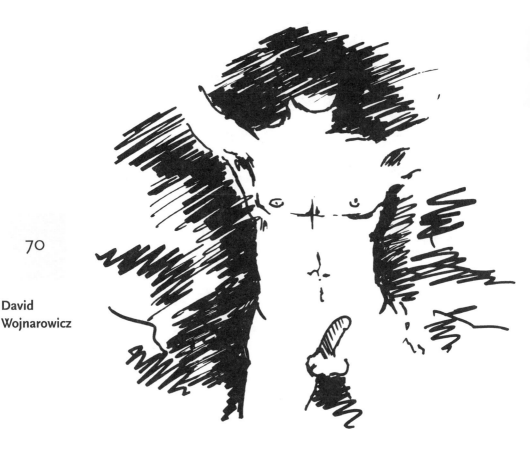

David
Wojnarowicz

7

I had an odd sleep last night. I felt like I was lying in a motel room for hours half awake or maybe I was just dreaming that I was half awake. In some part of my sleep I saw this fat little white worm, a grub-like thing that was no bigger than a quarter of an inch. When I leaned very close to it, my eye just centimeters above it, I could see every detail of the ridges of its flesh. It was a meat eater. The worm had latched onto something that looked like a goat fetus. It had large looping horns protruding from its head. The whole thing was white, fetal in appearance, its horns were translucent like fingernails. The grub was beginning to eat it and I pulled it off. It became very agitated and angry and tried to eat my fingers. I threw it onto the ground but there was yet another one and it was crawling toward some other fetal looking thing. I smacked it really hard. Picked it up and threw it down but my actions didn't kill it. My location was a wet dark hillside around dawn or dusk with a little light drifting over the land-scape. Looking around I realized that the entire contents of a biology lab or pet shop had been dumped on the ground. Maybe I had stolen everything. There were big black tarantulas, all sorts of lizards, some small mammals and bugs and frogs and snakes. At some point a big black tarantula was crawling around, blue-black and the size of a catcher's mitt. It made a little jump like it had seized something. I looked closely and saw it was eating an extraordinarily beautiful monitor lizard, a baby one. The spider didn't scare me; my sense of anxiety came from mixing the species. They all seemed to have come from different countries and were now thrown accidentally together by research or something. I pushed at the spider, picked it up and tried to unfasten its mandibles from the belly of the lizard. Someone else was with me; I handed them the spider and said, Take it somewhere else or put it in something until I figure out what I'm doing. The person threw the spider on the ground in a rough manner. I said, Don't do that, you'll kill it. If you drop a tarantula from a height higher than five inches its abdomen will burst.

8

Fevers. I wake up these mornings feeling wet like something from my soul, my memory is seeping out the back of my head onto the cloth of the pillows. I woke up earlier with intense nausea and headache. I turned on the television to try to get some focus outside my illness. Every station was filled with half-hour commercials disguised as talk shows in which low-grade tv actors and actresses talk about how to whiten your teeth or raise your investment earnings or shake the extra pounds from your bones. I am convinced I am from another planet. One station had a full closeup of a woman's face, middle-aged, saying, People talk about a sensation they've experienced when they are close to death in which their entire lives pass before their eyes. Well, you experience a similar moment when you are about to kill someone. You look at that person and see something in the moment before you kill him. You see his home, his family, his childhood, his hopes and beliefs, his sorrows and joys; all this passes before you in a flash. I didn't know what she was making these references for.

The nausea comes back. I try a new position on the bed with some pillows and slip back into sleep. I'm walking through this city not really sure where or why. I've got to piss really bad and go down this staircase of a subway or a hotel. (Architecture grows around my moving body like stone vegetation.) I find this old bathroom, mostly metal stalls and shadows like the subway station toilets of my childhood. I could sense sex as soon as I walked in, the moist scent of it in the yellow light and wet tiles and concrete. I go into this stall and pull out my dick and start pissing into the

**David
Wojnarowicz**

toilet. A big section of the stall's divider is peeled away and I see this guy
in his late teens early twenties jerking off watching me. When I finish I
reach through the partition and feel his chest through his shirt. He zips up
and comes around into my stall and closes the door and leans against it his
hands on his thighs. I unzip his trousers and peel them down to his knees.
I roll up his shirt so I can play with his belly. When his pants are down at
his knees I notice a fairly large wound on one of his thighs, lots of scrapes
and scratches on his body. The wound does something to me. I feel vaguely
nauseous but he is sexy enough to dispel it. He pulls down his underwear
and leans back again like he wants me to blow him. I crouch and slowly
start licking under the base of his prick. The wound is close to my eye and
I notice this series of red and green and yellow wires, miniature cables
looping out of it. There are two chrome cables with sectioned ribs pushing
under the sides of flesh. Then this blue glow coloring the air above the
wound. I stop licking and look closer and see it is a miniature monitor, a
tiny black and white television screen with an even tinier figure gesticulat-
ing from a podium in a vast room. There is the current president, smiling
like a corpse in a vigilante movie, addressing the nation on a live controlled
broadcast; the occasion is an enormous banquet in washington, a cannibal
banquet attended by heads of state and the usual cronies; kirkpatrick and
her biological warfare husband. The pope is seated next to buckley and his
sidekick buchanan. Oliver north is part of the entertainment and he squats

naked in a spotlight in the center of the ballroom floor. A small egg pops out of his ass and breaks in two on the floor. A tiny american flag tumbles out of the egg waving mechanically. The crowd breaks into wild applause as whitney houston steps forward to lead a rousing rendition of the star spangled banner. I wake up in a fever so delirious I am in a patriotic panic. Where, where the fuck at five in the morning could I run and buy a big american flag. My head hurts so bad I have to get out of bed and stand upright in order to ease the pressure. I go to the bathroom and finally throw up. I come back into the room, yank open the window and lean out above the dark empty streets and scream: THERE IS SOMETHING IN MY BLOOD AND IT'S TRYING TO FUCKING KILL ME.

9

I still fight the urge to puke. I've been fighting it all week. Whenever I witness signs of physical distress I have to fight the urge to bend over at the waist and empty out. It can be anything. The bum on the corner with festering sores on his face. It could be the moving skeleton I pass in the hall on the way in. Some guy with wasting syndrome and cmv blindness who is leaning precariously out his wheelchair in the unattended hallway searching in sightlessness for something he's lost. He's making braying sounds. What he's looking for is beneath the wheels of his chair. A tiny teddy bear with a collegiate outfit sewn to its body and a little flag glued to its paw. I pick it up and notice it has saliva and food matter stuck in its fur and I wonder if this is what civilization boils down to. I place it in the guy's hands and he squeals at me, his eyes a dull gray like the bellies of small fish. I have to resist the urge to puke. It's upsetting but I realize I'm only nauseated by my own mortality.

My friend on the bed is waking. The hospital gown has pulled up along his torso in the motions of sleep revealing a blobby looking penis and schools of cancer lesions twisting around his legs and abdomen. He opens his eyes too wide a couple of times and I hand him a bunch of flowers. I see double, he says. Twice as many flowers, I say.

10

Sometimes I come to hate people because they can't see where I am. I've gone empty, completely empty and all they see is the visual form; my arms and legs, my face, my height and posture, the sounds that come from my throat. But I'm fucking empty. The person I was just one year ago no longer exists; drifts spinning slowly into the ether somewhere way back there. I'm a xerox of my former self. I can't abstract my own dying any longer. I am a stranger to others and to myself and I refuse to pretend that I am familiar or that I have history attached to my heels. I am glass, clear empty glass. I see the world spinning behind and through me. I see casualness and mundane effects of gesture made by constant populations. I look familiar but I am a complete stranger being mistaken for my former selves. I am a stranger and I am moving. I am no longer animal vegetable or mineral. I am no longer made of circuits or discs. I am no longer coded and deciphered. I am all emptiness and futility. I am an empty stranger, a carbon copy of my form. I can no longer find what I'm looking for outside of myself. It doesn't exist out there. Maybe it's only in here, inside my head. But my head is glass and my eyes have stopped being cameras, the tape has run out and nobody's words can touch me. No gesture can touch me. I've been dropped into all this from another world and I can't speak your language any longer. See the signs I try to make with my hands and fingers. See the vague movements of my lips among the sheets. I'm a blank spot in a hectic civilization. I'm a dark smudge in the air that dissipates without notice. I feel like a window, maybe a broken window. I am a glass human. I am a glass human disappearing in rain. I am standing among all of you waving my invisible arms and hands. I am shouting my invisible words. I am getting so weary. I am growing tired. I am waving to you from here. I am crawling around looking for the aperture of complete and final emptiness. I am vibrating in isolation among you. I am screaming but it comes out like pieces of clear ice. I am signaling that the volume of all this is too high. I am waving. I am waving my hands. I am disappearing. I am disappearing but not fast enough.

David
Wojnarowicz

Anal Pleasure and the Anal Taboo
from *Anal Pleasure and Health:*
A Guide for Men and Women

JACK MORIN

In this era of sexual exploration, attitudes toward the anus and anal pleasure are still, to a large extent, governed by the processes of taboo. Taboo is
a form of psycho-social control more potent than even the most rigid
moral code. Modern societies are in the habit of believing that the scientific method has eradicated taboos and that only "primitive" peoples are
still affected by them.

This is not altogether true. While science has been instrumental in
freeing us from many irrational ideas and fears, our culture, like all others,
nonetheless still has its taboos. A taboo is a prohibition collectively shared
by a society, with a force so strong that it is rarely questioned or even discussed. *It just is.* Every society has rules, laws or principles intended to
guide or control behavior. These grow out of general systems of values
shared by most members of the culture. Taboos are different. Sigmund
Freud made this important distinction:

> The taboo restrictions are different from religious or moral prohibi-
> tions; they are differentiated from moral prohibitions by failing to
> be included in a system which declares abstinence in general to be
> necessary and gives reasons for this necessity. The taboo prohibi-
> tions lack all justification and are of unknown origin...[They] are
> taken as a matter of course by those under their dominance (Freud,
> 1913).

Taboos, then, have an all-encompassing quality—like the air we breathe—
which makes them highly resistant to logic, scientific inquiry or even experience. Although taboos obviously do develop from within a culture, it is as

if they are imposed from beyond it. For instance, in the Judeo-Christian tradition, the taboo against anal intercourse is seen as coming from God. In the Old Testament story, God completely destroys the city of Sodom, presumably as punishment for rampant sodomy among its people. Many scholars now believe that the punishment was for Sodom's violation of hospitality rules, and had little, if anything, to do with sex. The sodomy interpretation, however, is still the one generally accepted. Among believers, condemnation of anal sex is not based on any discernible principle except the desire to avoid the wrath of God.

Some taboos are readily taken for granted by virtually everyone in the culture with little or no ambivalence or emotional charge. The taboo against eating the meat of dogs or cats is of this type. We are socialized to feel that this would be distasteful and the issue never arises again. If, however, we were to find ourselves in a situation where no other food was available except a dog or cat, we would be thrown into deep ambivalence. Some people would probably come close to death before violating the taboo.

Other taboos tend to be accompanied by strong ambivalence and a high emotional charge. The incest taboo is the best example of this type. Because everyone at some time has sexual feelings toward their parents, and vice versa, the taboo against acting upon or even feeling these desires has even greater psychological significance. Early sexual feelings toward mother, father, sisters or brothers are almost certainly pleasurable. The feeling of pleasure versus the taboo throws the person into a state of ambivalence, until the ambivalence is itself repressed with varying degrees of success.

Both types of taboos have a chilling effect upon behavior and thought. However, taboos of the second type never really eliminate the behaviors and feelings they forbid. Instead, these desires go "underground," both individually and collectively, where they take on a bigger-than-life, almost cosmic significance. In this way, a taboo gives the forbidden feeling or behavior an inflated significance. In turn, the ambivalence and guilt which a person feels are intensified even further.* Freud pointed out that in Polynesian the root meaning of taboo is *both* sacred *and* forbidden or unclean. The opposite of taboo is simply ordinary, common or readily accessible.

All of this applies to the feelings of most people in our culture toward the anal area and anal pleasure. There is no other way to understand the frequent responses of rational men and women, even scientists, when asked

* This was a central issue in the theoretical conflict between Sigmund Freud and Carl Jung. Freud thought that strong incestuous desires were an inevitable psychic occurrence. Jung, on the other hand, thought that the incest taboo itself, in combination with guilt about sexual desires, intensified incestuous feelings.

Jack Morin

straightforward questions about the anus and anal pleasure, especially anal sex. More often than not they are unwilling to discuss the subject in any detail or are repulsed by the very idea. Often the effects of the anal taboo are hidden under a few simple rational-sounding arguments (e.g., anal intercourse is medically dangerous), which fail to meet even minimal standards of logic or scientific investigation. If anal pleasure and eroticism were simply a bad idea, objections (whether moral, legal or physiological) could be discussed without embarrassment. In actuality, it seems that most people can more comfortably discuss murder and rape than anal pleasure.

Like the incest taboo, the anal taboo tends to be highly charged, though usually not as strong. This is true because the sensitivity of the anal area assures that beginning early in life virtually everyone will receive pleasurable sensations from the anus. To some degree, then, negative messages about the anus are bound to contradict actual experience. Because of the strength of the pleasurable sensations and the strength of the negative messages, some degree of ambivalence is inevitable. For some, the discomfort of mixed feelings can be partially avoided by suppressing all thoughts and feelings related to anal pleasure. This is the most common reaction. Others are clearly interested *and* repulsed, fascinated *and* guilty about anal pleasure, especially anal eroticism.

Charged by the excitement of the forbidden, a few people become anal enthusiasts, ascribing tremendous importance to anal sex. This can be a problem for those who feel that the more forbidden or "naughty" a sexual behavior or fantasy is, the more important it becomes, as a matter of principle, to do it. Such men and women often engage in anal sex as a symbol of open-mindedness, whether they actually like it or not. This is an example of how a taboo—and subsequent reactions to it—tend to exaggerate or distort the significance of the forbidden behaviors and feelings. Taboo behaviors and thoughts, whatever they happen to be, then assume a looming importance that both expresses and perpetuates the taboo.

In the context of taboo, clouded by the crossfire of conflicting extremes, it becomes very difficult clearly to recognize the forbidden object or behavior or to make a decision as to whether the forbidden object or behavior has anything of value to offer. The emotions generated by a violation of the taboo become the focus of attention. The behavior behind the taboo is likely to be all but ignored in the struggle.

Social Functions of the Anal Taboo

Taboos are not just psychological phenomena. They have social significance as well. The incest taboo, for example, functions to help reduce severe conflict among family members and between generations. The taboo against eating dog and cat meat functions to maintain the special feelings people wish to have about their pets. The functions of a taboo are not always clearly discernible. They become blurred as the taboo is passed from generation to generation. As a taboo becomes intricately woven into the collective psyche, its original significance may be lost. The anal taboo has never been systematically studied by social scientists. Nonetheless, it is possible to speculate about its social functions. Cross-cultural data about sexual mores and behavior strongly point to four likely functions.

First, negative attitudes toward the anal area appear to be universally tied to concerns about cleanliness. All societies encourage cleanliness, though ideas about what is required vary widely. Relatively few cultures are as compulsive about these matters as Americans tend to be. Yet the idea that cleanliness is necessary for spiritual purity (i.e., "next to godliness") is not unusual. Often, symbols of cleanliness, or dirtiness, serve as focal points of intense significance. Specific substances like certain foods, mud, urine, mucus, and feces trigger strong feelings of revulsion, thereby symbolizing the much broader concern about cleanliness. The anal taboo functions in this way. By becoming symbolic of all that is unclean, and fostering the emotion of disgust, the anus and feces serve to focus and intensify the value placed on being clean.

Second, the idea that an inherent conflict exists between the spirit and the body is prevalent. This notion is certainly strong in all Judeo-Christian societies. By intensifying negative emotions about one area of the body, the anal taboo expresses and perpetuates a more general mistrust of the body. It makes concrete the conflict between spirit and body, increases guilt, and thereby reinforces religious doctrine.

Third, almost all cultures associate receiving anal intercourse with femininity, probably because of its physiological similarity to vaginal intercourse. With few exceptions, a man who receives anal intercourse is viewed as less manly. Therefore, another possible function of the anal taboo is the maintenance of strict sex-role differentiation. Sexual receptivity—and all that it symbolizes—is expected of women and strongly discouraged in men. If anal pleasure is prohibited, then, the chances of men receiving anal intercourse decrease considerably.

Finally, acceptance of anal sexual behavior is virtually always correlated with acceptance of some forms of homosexuality. It therefore seems reasonable to conclude that another function of the anal taboo is to bolster sanctions against homosexual behavior, particularly among men.

From these perspectives, this time in history is ripe for challenging the anal taboo. Scientific advances in the study of health and disease make it more possible for decisions about cleanliness to be rational rather than emotional, although emotions still do and probably always will play an

78

Jack Morin

important part. The split between mind/body is being directly challenged in philosophy, psychology and even medicine. Similarly, the value of strict sex-role differentiation is being questioned by both women and men. At the same time, negative attitudes toward homosexuality are beginning slowly to change. For all these reasons, the functions the anal taboo once served may no longer hold such significance.

Those who wish to counter the long, complex effects of the anal taboo must focus on two central questions: One, what can the role of the anal area be in healthy, self-affirming, sensual and sexual activity when freed from the stranglehold of taboo? Two, how can people go about freeing themselves from the taboo? This book is intended to help you investigate these questions and find your own answers.

Anal Pleasure
and the Anal
Taboo

Egg Sex
from *Susie Bright's Sexual Reality:*
A Virtual Sex World Reader

SUSIE BRIGHT

In 1966, when I was eight years old, my mother gave me a little pink book, *A Baby Is Born.* In great detail, and with lots of close-ups and diagrams, it described exactly what a sperm and egg looked like and how they joined together, with subsequent portraits of the developing fetus.

How did the sperm meet the egg to begin with? The book said simply "Mommy and Daddy love each other very much. They lie close together and, after performing intercourse, the sperm is on its way to fertilize the egg." There was no accompanying diagram, so I made what was probably my first earnest attempt to read between the lines of any piece of literature. I gleaned nothing.

Twenty-five years later, I was pregnant, and this time I went out and bought my own collection of pink and blue books bulging with instruction for prospective parents. Of course, there was a great deal to learn about fetal development and breast-feeding techniques, but I couldn't help but check each index under "Sexuality—during and after pregnancy." All the manuals, from Dr. Spock to the latest yuppie know-how, followed an almost identical script: "Mommy and Daddy love each other very much...." Following this vein, the paragraphs on sexuality gave advice that was inexplicit, vague, and almost threatening in their avoidance of the nitty-gritty.

Steeped in a romance-novel notion of marriage, sexual advice to pregnant moms, whether revealed in print or in the strange silences at the doctor's office, gives short shrift to the dramatic changes in women's sexual physiology and desires. Great emphasis is placed on how to cope with the ambivalent husband's feelings towards his wife's body and the burden pregnancy puts on their normal sexual routine.

None of these books was written in the sixties. All of them glow with feminist and holistic approaches to mothering, supporting working moms, refuting the sexist prejudices against breast-feeding, and offering all manner of enlightened positive self-esteem for the mother-to-be. I began to wonder if anyone *knew* what went on in women's sexual lives during pregnancy. The most definitive statement the books managed was: Sometimes she's hot, sometimes she's not. This wouldn't be the first time that traditional medicine had nothing to contribute to an understanding of female sexuality.

Meanwhile, my clit started to grow. Everyone knows that a pregnant woman's breasts swell in accompaniment to her belly, but why had no one told me that my genitals would also grow? My vulva engorged with blood; my labia grew fatter; my clit pushed slightly out of its hood. I was reading absolutely everything on the subject of pregnant sex by this point and, by picking out the fragments of pertinent information, I learned I was not peculiar in this regard.

It's a little embarrassing to be thirty-one years old and finally get the message that my primary and secondary sexual characteristics are not simply for display and petting. I was being physically and psychologically dominated by the life growing inside me, and of course I wanted both to escape and to submit. I was unusually sensual and amorous, and yet, twenty weeks into pregnancy, I found I could not successfully masturbate the way I had been doing since I was a kid. I was stunned and a little panicky. My engorged clitoris was different under my fingers; too sensitive to touch my usual way, and what other way was there?

That's when it hit me. The experts all say that it is a mystery why some women get more horny when they're pregnant while others lose interest. I'll tell you something—no one loses interest. What happens is that your normal sexual patterns don't work the same way anymore. Unless you and your lover make the transition to new ways of getting excited and reaching orgasms, you are going to be very depressed about sex and start avoiding it all together.

It's not just a technique change, either. Feeling both desirable *and* protected are essential to a pregnant woman, and if protection is not forthcoming from the outside, she will build a fortress that cannot be penetrated.

I no longer believe that some women don't feel sexual during those long nine months. Some are frightened by the sexual changes their growing bodies demand. But so many others confided to me, "I was so hot, and I couldn't explain it to just anyone."

It's an awesome feat of American Puritanism to convince us that sex and pregnancy do not mix. It's the ultimate virgin/whore distinction. For those nine months, please don't mention how we got this way—we're Mary now.

Egg Sex

Your average Mary's physical transformation is quite different from an immaculate conception. A woman's vagina changes when she is pregnant, much like her vulva and clit. The lubrication increases; its smell and texture are different. Often exhibiting a pregnancy-type yeast infection, her genitals smell like a big cookie.

When I fucked during my pregnancy, I felt like I was participating in a slow elastic taffy pull. I was more passive sexually than ever before, with no ambition to strap one on, or get on top, or do much of anything besides take it all in and float. I was one gigantic egg cozy.

Truthfully, you don't get gigantic for at least five or six months. The advice books make much controversy over positions for intercourse, but I didn't find positioning to be that big a deal. It's typical of mainstream sex books to focus on "positions" in the masculine way one might prepare a sports manual. You can fuck on your back for a long time if you like, as long as your partner doesn't insist on collapsing upon you. Flat on one's belly is of course impossible after six months, but slightly turned to the side works just fine. It is often recommended that the woman get on top, but as I said, I couldn't be bothered.

Sex is also a crucial way to prepare for childbirth. Start with the premise that birth is the biggest sex act you will ever take part in, and everything will flow from that. If you are smart and take childbirth preparation classes, you may even get a teacher who knows something about the sexual side of birth.

My teacher was very subtle. She gave us an almost unreadable handout in the fourth month, an instruction sheet for an exercise called "perineal massage." I thought of my perineum, the little inch of skin running between my vagina and my anus. How could rubbing something the size of a birthday candle help me in labor?

The flyer (which opened, of course, with the obligatory spiel: "Mommy and Daddy love each other very much...") said that Daddy should massage and finger the vaginal opening until he could put more and more of his fingers inside, relaxing the vaginal muscles through such caresses until he might be able to press a small orange or even his whole hand into Mommy's opening.

His whole hand! I called up one of my friends who has the breadth of experience as both a mother of two and a retired porn star. "Is 'perineal massage' really fist fucking?" I asked her.

"Of course," she said, laughing, "and it really helps."

I could see why immediately. A hand going inside my pussy is a little like a baby's head trying to move outside into the world. How exciting! For the first time, I felt a surge of confidence about my chances for a successful labor. Since I had practiced fisting, clearly I was in great shape for the real thing.

82

Susie Bright

Perineal massage is not discussed in every hospital or prenatal setting. Most couples and their care providers are steeped in the dominance of penis-vagina intercourse. It requires a different sort of orientation to devote attention to the possibilities of fingers and hands. But with a little encouragement and a flyer with pictures and plain English, I think more parents would enjoy the intense relaxation and vulnerability that comes with fisting, or "oranging," if you prefer.

I pestered my teacher for three weeks about whether she thought using a vibrator during labor would be helpful for pain relief. She said each time that we would discuss it next week. She recommended all sorts of other distractions and exercises: going to the bathroom frequently, changing positions, getting in the bathtub, focusing on a special object, etc. Well, I decided on my own that my Hitachi magic wand was going to be my focus object. I believed that stimulating my clit could be a nice counterpoint to the contractions going on inside my belly.

I have a great photograph of me in the delivery room, dilated to six centimeters, with a blissful look on my face and my vibrator nestled against my pubic bone. I had not thought of climaxing, but the pleasure of the rhythm on my clit was like sweet icing on top of the deep, thick contractions in my womb. I would have been too tired and distracted to touch myself with my fingers at that point, and the power cord was just one of about ten that the doctors had coming from my bed. Due to my baby's unusual breech position, I had a complicated birth that finally ended in an emergency Cesarean. But I had a great labor.

My friend Barbara confessed to me after her first child that she had never been so turned on in her life. When the baby's head was crowning, she called out to her husband over and over, "I want to come, touch me, please touch me!"—and he thought she was hysterical.

We are utterly unaccustomed to seeing birthing as a sexual experience. A lot of us think of childbirth as something close to death; at least, that's what I was afraid of. I heard women screaming in the rooms next to me at the hospital and I knew those screams weren't exclusively from physical pain, but from wild, wild fear. It's terribly frightening when you don't know what your body is doing and when your sexuality is divorced from this incredible process. Being afraid makes the pain much worse and makes your stamina unknowable.

There was a traffic jam of births at the city hospitals the week I had my daughter. It was about nine months after the big earthquake hit San Francisco, and apparently staying home had been a fertile pastime during that otherwise sobering period. The other women who had children the day and night I was in the hospital did not appear to have husbands at their sides. It was easy for me to imagine their stories: they were single;

 83

Egg Sex

they were lesbians; they had husbands who didn't want to see them that way; they had husbands who had left them earlier in their pregnancies; they had husbands in the service and far away.

I didn't read a single parenting book that reflected any of these lives, although they are as common place as conception itself. The fractured fairy tale ("Mommy and Daddy love each other very much") is only resonant in the sense that parents need to be loved and nurtured, because they are about to give of themselves in a way that they never dreamed possible before.

If the mother doesn't receive tenderness and passion during her nine months, the bitterness she develops lasts well beyond childbirth—her kids will know all about it. Perhaps I could encourage childbirth professionals to advocate good sex during pregnancy as a key to psychologically healthy children.

Susie Bright

After the birth, you will get doctor's instructions to abstain from sex for the next six weeks. We've all heard the woman who says, "I don't care if I don't have sex for the next six years." But if her pussy is so sore, why can't she enjoy oral sex? Her breasts are leaking colostrum, ready to start expressing milk, and they need to be sucked by someone who knows about sucking breasts—babies don't always get the hang of it instantly, or at Mom's command.

The truth is, this six weeks rule is arbitrary, and it's based on the fear of an infection resulting from a man ejaculating inside the vagina. There is a lot more to "sex" than this. Nothing magic happens at the end of six weeks. Not everyone's os and vaginal passageway are in the same condition after birth. Having had a Cesarean, mine had not been through a full-blown vaginal birth. Without knowing exactly what risk I was taking, but knowing that the doctor didn't know what he was talking about either, I came home from the hospital and made love on the sixth day after my daughter was born.

I've spoken with many women who admitted the same. "My husband and I had waited so long for this child," said my nurse practitioner/mid-wife, who had a child after she was forty, "that we had to be intimate right away." I appreciated her using the word "intimate," because I don't think it's the case that you just have this wild hare to get it on once the baby is born. You want a closeness, a release, and a celebration that you haven't necessarily experienced during labor.

My midwife also told me that she started asking her patients how soon after childbirth they had resumed intercourse. Lots of people break the rules, as you can imagine, and she found that women who had intercourse earlier on also resumed periods much sooner than those who waited. This little discovery—from a professional who wouldn't ordinarily tell me such things—reminded me again how little we know because no one shares taboo information.

Nursing is another source of mixed feelings, erotic and otherwise. One woman winces in pain from chapped and bleeding nipples, while another has orgasms from her baby's suckling. Again, if these things were brought out in the open, a lot of nipple soreness would disappear. Breast feeding does *not* come instinctively, and it helps to have someone show you as well as tell you how to nurse comfortably.

I was satisfied just to nurse my baby competently. My erotic feelings came not so much from my baby's sucking as from feeling my breasts express themselves at other times. Sexual arousal will make your breasts leak when you're lactating, another important fact missing in most parent handbooks. As much as I have lectured on G-spot orgasms, I had never had anything come *out* of me when I was making love before, and this made my head swim with embarrassment at first and then arousal.

Egg Sex

I've always been one of those women who could be secretive about her climax. I could come without crying out. I could be very sneaky. Having my nipples not just stiffen, but release milk like a faucet every time I was turned on took me for a very un-private loop. But I loved rubbing it on my lover's chest, or my own. I felt some feminine equivalent of virility, making the biggest wet spot of them all. This was the very opposite of being hooked up to the electric breast pump, which made me feel like a working cow. Handy, but totally unerotic.

It would be unfair to conclude the erotic disposition of pregnancy without talking about changes in sexual fantasies. Our fantasies often seem to be written in stone at an early age and are not too easily transformed in our adult years. But having a baby is the next big hormone explosion a woman can have after puberty, and she may surprise herself with what comes to mind at the moment of orgasm. I did.

In retrospect I see that my fantasy life during my pregnancy was cathartic. One of my biggest and most irrational reservations about having a child (besides fearing that I would die in childbirth) was that if I had a boy, I wouldn't know how to raise him. I would be a disaster, whether teaching him how to use the toilet or to fly a kite. Petty sexual stereotypes aside, I didn't know what little boys were like. I have no brothers, was raised by my mom, and always preferred dresses.

I'm a single parent, but I had conversations with the father of my kid now and then during my pregnancy. He was concerned that I was planning a politically correct dress code for the young one. "If it's a girl, I suppose you'll make her wear pants," he pouted.

"Oh no," I said. "If I have a little girl, I'm going to make sure she has the frilliest, laciest, puffiest dresses you ever saw," remembering the kind of dresses I always wanted.

"And if it's a little boy," he started.

"Of course," I interrupted, "He'll have the frilliest, laciest, puffiest…"

My teasing was just a cover. I really didn't know what little boys were supposed to wear.

One night, I was making love with my friend, John, and I imagined that he was my son. I came like a rocket, and I didn't have the nerve to tell him about it for weeks. In the meantime, I could not get this image off my mind. I recalled a really tacky porn movie I had seen years ago, *Taboo*, where beautiful mom Kay Parker has a son (in real life, a grown-up actor named Mike Ranger) who only has eyes for her. I wasn't aroused by the movie the first time I saw it, but now this scene could turn me on instantly. I couldn't masturbate or make love to anyone, man or woman, without conjuring up this incestuous exchange.

Susie Bright

At the same time, while making my plans for the baby and talking to friends and family, I was noticeably more at ease about having a boy child. I didn't know what sex my baby was, and unlike so many other moms, I didn't want to know.

I started noticing mothers with their sons on the street, and I didn't panic; I smiled at them. Somebody gave me a book on how to be a "dad," with all sorts of fabulous hints on butch activities from skipping stones to throwing a ball. I read the whole thing and thought it was a blast. I asked all my friends how many of them had fathers who did any of these things, and our answers shed a lot of light on our gender points of view.

When my team of doctors finally pulled Aretha from my womb, they were exuberant. "It's a girl!" somebody said. I was shaking very badly from the anesthesia, but this warm little yolk of feeling spilled in my head, and tears of relief came to my eyes. I was so pleased to have a daughter.

When I came home and had my first chance to fantasize (something sleep deprivation cut into quite a bit), I could not for the life of me conjure up my imaginary son! He had split. My incest fantasy had expressed my fear of having a boy, and when that possibility disappeared, the fantasy lost its magic. I don't know what would have happened to my fantasy if I had indeed come home with a son. I think I would have moved on, just as I did after Aretha's birth, to new sets of anxieties which became fresh erotic fodder.

Now I fantasize about being pregnant again—talk about kinky. In reality I have no desire to be eating soda crackers for a month and having to go to the bathroom every ten minutes for the next half year. But I do have glowing memories of the sexual discoveries I made during pregnancy, and I'm grateful I had a sexually loving and inquisitive support system around me. If the whole process could be like that…. Well, maybe I'll have another one, I tell myself, when my daughter is old enough to change the diapers.

Brother to Brother: Words from the Heart from *In the Life: A Black Gay Anthology*

JOSEPH BEAM

…what is most important to me must be spoken, made verbal and shared, even at the risk of having it bruised or misunderstood.[1]

I know the anger that lies inside me like I know the beat of my heart and the taste of my spit. It is easier to be angry than to hurt. Anger is what I do best. It is easier to be furious than to be yearning. Easier to crucify myself in you than to take on the threatening universe of whiteness by admitting that we are worth wanting each other.[2]

I, too, know anger. My body contains as much anger as water. It is the material from which I have built my house: blood red bricks that cry in the rain. It is what pulls my tie and gold chains taut around my neck; fills my penny loafers and my Nikes; molds my Calvins and gray flannels to my torso. It is the face and posture I show the world. It is the way, sometimes the only way, I am granted an audience. It is sometimes the way I show affection. I am angry because of the treatment I am afforded as a Black man. That fiery anger is stoked additionally with the fuels of contempt and despisal shown me by my community because I am gay. *I cannot go home as who I am.*

When I speak of home, I mean not only the familial constellation from which I grew, but the entire Black community: the Black press, the Black church, Black academicians, the Black literati, and the Black left. Where is my reflection? I am most often rendered invisible, perceived as a threat to the family, or am tolerated if I am silent and inconspicuous. I cannot go home as who I am and that hurts me deeply.

Almost every morning I have coffee at the same donut shop. Almost every morning I encounter the same Black man who used to acknowledge me from across the counter. I can only surmise that it is my earrings and earcuffs that have tipped him off that I am gay. He no longer speaks, instead looks disdainfully through me as if I were glass. But glass reflects, so I am not even that. He sees no part of himself in me—not my Blackness nor my maleness. "There's nothing in me that is not in everyone else, and nothing in everyone else that is not in me."[3] Should our glances meet, he is quick to use his *Wall Street Journal* as a shield while I wince and admire the brown of my coffee in my cup.

I do not expect his approval—only his acknowledgment. The struggles of Black people are too perilous and too pervasive for us to dismiss one another, in such cursory fashion, because of perceived differences. Gil Scott-Heron called it "dealing in externals," that is, giving great importance to visual information and ignoring real aspects of commonality. Aren't all hearts and fists and minds needed in this struggle or will this faggot be tossed into the fire? In this very critical time everyone from the corner to the corporation is desperately needed.

**Joseph
Beam**

> ...[Brother] the war goes on
> respecting no white flags
> taking no prisoners
> giving no time out for women and children
> to leave the area
> whether we return their fire
> or not
> whether we're busy attacking each other
> or not.[4]

If you could put your newspaper aside for a moment, I think you, too, would remember that it has not always been this way between us. I remember. I remember the times before different meant separate, before different meant outsider. I remember Sunday school and backyard barbecues and picnics in the Park and the Avenue and parties in dimly lit basements and skateboards fashioned from two-by-fours and b-ball and...
I remember. I also recall secretly playing jacks and jumping rope on the back porch, and the dreams I had when I spent the night at your house.

But that was before different meant anything at all, certainly anything substantial. That was prior to considerations such as too light/too dark; or good/bad hair; before college/army/jail; before working/middle class; before gay/straight. But I am no longer content on the back porch; I want to play with my jacks on the front porch. There is no reason for me to hide.

Our differences should promote dialogue rather than erect new obstacles in our paths.

On another day: I am walking down Spruce/Castro/Christopher Street on my way to work. A half block away, walking towards me, is another Black gay man. We have seen each other in the clubs. Side by side, and at the precise moment that our eyes should meet, he studies the intricate detail of a building. I check my white sneakers for scuff marks. What is it that we see in each other that makes us avert our eyes so quickly? Does he see the same thing in me that the brother in the donut shop sees? Do we turn away from each other in order not to see our collective anger and sadness?

It is my pain I see reflected in your eyes. Our angers ricochet between us like the bullets we fire in battles which are not our own nor with each other.

The same angry face, donned for safety in the white world, is the same expression I bring to you. I am cool and unemotive, distant from what I need most. "It is easier to be furious than to be yearning. Easier to crucify myself in you..." And perhaps easiest to ingest that anger until it threatens to consume me, or apply a salve of substitutes to the wound.

But real anger accepts few substitutes and sneers at sublimation. The anger-hurt I feel cannot be washed down with a Coke (old or new) or a Colt 45; cannot be danced away; cannot be mollified by a white lover, nor lost in the mirror reflections of a Black lover; cannot evaporate like sweat after a Nautilus workout; nor drift away in a cloud of reefer smoke. I cannot leave it in Atlantic City, or Rio, or even Berlin when I vacation. I cannot hope it will be gobbled up by the alligators on my clothing; nor can I lose it in therapeutic catharsis. I cannot offer it to Jesus/Allah/Jah. So, I must mold and direct that fiery cool mass of angry energy—use it before it uses me! *Anger unvented becomes pain, pain unspoken becomes rage, rage released becomes violence.*

Use it to create a Black gay community in which I can build my home surrounded by institutions that reflect and sustain me. Concurrent with that vision is the necessity to repave the road home, widening it, so I can return with all I have created to the home which is my birthright.

II

Silence is what I hear after the handshake and the slap of five; after the salutations: what's happenin'/what's up/how you feel; after our terms of endearment: homeboy, cuzz, "girlfriend," blood, running buddy, and Miss Thing. I can hear the silence. When talking with a "girlfriend," I am more likely to muse about my latest piece or so-and-so's party at Club She-She than about the anger and hurt I felt that morning when a jeweler refused me entrance to his store because I am Black and male, and we are all perceived as thieves. I will swallow that hurt and should I speak of it, will vocalize only the anger, saying: I have bust out his fuckin' windows! Some of the anger will be exorcised, but the hurt, which has not been given voice, prevails and accumulates.

Silence is a way to grin and bear it. A way not to acknowledge how much my life is discounted each day—100% OFF ALL BLACK MEN TODAY—EVERY DAY! I strive to appear strong and silent. I learn to ingest hatred at a geometric rate and to count (silently) to ten thousand… ten million. But as I have learned to mute my cries of anguish, so have I learned to squelch my exclamations of joy. What remains is the rap.

**Joseph
Beam**

My father is a warm brown man of seventy, who was born in Barbados. He is kind and gentle, and has worked hard for me so that I am able to write these words. We are not friends: he is my father, I am his son. We are silent when alone together. I do not ask him about his island childhood or his twelve years as a janitor or about the restaurant he once owned where he met my mother. He does not ask me about being gay or why I wish to write about it. Yet we are connected: his past is my present, our present a foundation for the future. I have never said to him that his thick callused hands have led me this far and given me options he never dreamed of. How difficult it is to speak of my appreciation, saying: Dad, I love you. *I am here because of you, much deeper than sperm meeting egg, much deeper than sighs in the night, I am here because of you.* Our love for each other, though great, may never be spoken. It is the often unspoken love that Black men give to other Black men in a world where we are forced to cup our hands over our mouths or suffer under the lash of imprisonment, unemployment, or even death. But these words, which fail, are precisely the words that are life-giving and continuing. They must be given voice. What legacy is to be found in our silence?

Because of the silence among us, each one of us, as Black boys and men maturing, must all begin the struggle to survive anew. With the incomplete knowledge of what has gone before, our struggles to endure and maintain, at best, save us only as individuals. Collectively we falter and stumble, covering up our experiences in limp aphorisms: Times are hard! Watch out for the Man! This is the depth of the sage advice we offer each other—at arm's length. We must begin to speak of our love and concern for each other as vigorously as we argue party politics or the particular merits of an athletic team.

Daydream: 29 April 1984
Today was the first beautiful day that I have not had to spend at

work. Precisely the kind of day I want to share with a lover: gazing at the blue sky; making love in the western sunlight on the brown-sheeted bed; massaging each other with the musk oil that warms on the window sill. We'd shower together, and return to the bed to dry in the sunlight as we had sweated when we made love.

Today, I think also of Bryan, and of myself as the hopeless romantic that I sometimes am. How can I be so taken with you, boy-man, who I met only two weeks ago? Why is it that I want to share all my waking moments with you? Share my world with you? Protect you? Tell you things no one told me when I was twenty-two. You are like the little brother I never had; the playmates I was not sup-posed to touch. You are the lover who is considerate; the son I will not issue, eyes bright and inquisitive. I want to hold you the way my father never held me. I want to know your face, the oily brown-ness of your skin: its shadows, the darkness around the elbows and under the buttocks. I daydream of brown-on-brown-on-brown.

I am at a poetry reading. The brother at the podium is reading a poem about his running buddy who was killed in Vietnam. At the gravesite of his dead friend, the poet reminisces about the big fun they'd had, sharing bot-tles of wine and hanging on the corner. Only when everyone has gone and he stares at the mound of dirt that covers his homeboy, can he utter: "Man, I really loved you. I really, really loved you."

Why does it take us so long?

I, too, have been there. Two good high school buddies died within a year of our graduation: Chris in a charter plane crash on his way back to college; Steve of a heart attack while playing basketball. We were all nine-teen and assumed life would go on. There seemed to be no rush to speak of how we cherished one another's friendship. I was away at college when they were both buried; I will always regret that silence.

We have few traditions like those of Black women. No kitchen tables around which to assemble. No intimate spaces in which to explore our feel-ings of love and friendship. No books like *The Color Purple*. We gather in public places: barber shops, bars, lodges, fraternities, and street corners, places where bravado rather than intimacy are the rule. We assemble to do something rather than *be* with each other. We can talk about the Man, but not about how we must constantly vie with one another for the scant crumbs thrown our way. We can talk about dick and ass and pussy, but not of the fierce competition for too few jobs and scholarships. We can talk about sporting events in amazing detail, but not about how we are pitted, one against the other, as permanent adversaries.

Dream: 15 February 1984
We have all gathered in the largest classroom I have ever been in.
Black men of all kinds and colors. We sit and talk and listen, telling
the stories of our lives. All of the things we have ever wanted to say
to each other but did not. There is much laughter but also many
tears. Why has it taken us so long? Our silence has hurt us so much.

III

**Joseph
Beam**

Dreams are what propel us through life, and allow us to focus above and
beyond the hurdles that dot our passage. Medger, Martin, and Malcolm
were dreamers. And they were killed. I dare myself to dream. If I cannot
vocalize a dream, which is the first step towards its realization, then I have
no dream. It remains a thought, a vision without form. I dare myself to
dream that our blood is thicker than difference.

In the fall of 1980, I did not know that one of every four Black men would
experience prison in his lifetime. Nor did I know that my motivation for
writing to prisoners arose from a deep sense of my captivity as a closeted
gay man and an oppressed Black man, rather than as an act of righteous-
ness. Finally, I had no idea that such a correspondence would become an
integral part of my life and a place for dreaming.

Ombaka and I began writing to each other under unusual circumstances. I had been writing to another prisoner named Morris, who had
been transferred or released, but, in any case, had vacated the particular
cell, which was to be Ombaka's new home. Ombaka found my last letter to
Morris, read it, and responded. He apologized profusely in that first letter
about how contrary it was to prison etiquette to read someone else's mail
and even ruder to respond to it. Almost four years, and forty letters later, it
seems ironic that this friendship, one of the most important in my life, is
the result of such a chance occurrence. More ironic and sadder is that we
probably would not have met any other way; we are that different.

I am gay and from the north; he is straight and from the south. I'm an
agnostic; he's a Muslim. When I was attending prep school, Ombaka was
busily acquiring his street smarts. While I studied in college, he was finish-
ing his stint in the Army. When I was beginning graduate school, he had
just begun his prison sentence. Under other circumstances these differences might have separated us. What could have been used as weapons of
castigation became tools of sharing.

Our initial letters were filled with the tentative gestures one employs
with new friends, the shyness, the formality, and the small talk. We

searched for common ground for dialogue and the soft spots to be avoided. We spoke of the advantages and disadvantages of street smarts versus formal education. We talked at length about sexuality and how we became the sexual beings that we are. We discussed our use of language: I greatly admired his rural tongue with its graceful turn of phrase, which seemed more natural than my stilted style, which he respected. He told me of his experiences as a Muslim and as a father; I related tales from college and gay life in the big city. We talked and talked about our differences, but we also gave each other permission to dream and to speak of those dreams. What an exciting yet fearful prospect, dreaming in the open.

Black dreams are dashed as assuredly as Black dreamers are killed. We are allowed to dream of being athletes, entertainers, and lotto winners. These are the dreams which have been dreamt for us to maintain us just where we are. How little support there is, from one another or from society, for dreams borne of personal conviction and desire. I dare myself to dream.

Brother to Brother: Words from the Heart

Astronaut Guy Bluford and I grew up on the same block. It was no secret that he dreamed of being an astronaut, but in the early sixties it was difficult for little Black boys to imagine being anything other than what we had seen. And we had seen no Black astronauts nor Black mayors of major U.S. cities. We all thought Bluford was crazy, but his dreams became a reality. We can dream the dark, the seemingly impossible.

Ombaka and I dreamt of being writers. During the course of our correspondence we *became* writers. Several months ago he sent me a 260-page manuscript of his first novel, and I am beginning to work on a major writing project (this anthology). I am extremely happy that our friendship was not lost to anger, or silence, or perceived differences. I dare myself to dream.

I dare myself to dream of us moving from survival to potential, from merely getting by to a positive getting over. I dream of Black men loving and supporting other Black men, and relieving Black women from the role of primary nurturers in our community. I dream, too, that as we receive more of what we want from each other that our special anger reserved for Black women will disappear. For too long have we expected from Black women that which we could only obtain from other men. I dare myself to dream.

I dream of a time when it is not Black men who fill the nation's prisons; when we will not seek solace in a bottle and Top papers; and when the service is not the only viable alternative to high civilian unemployment.

I dare myself to dream of a time when I will pass a group of brothers on the corner, and the words "fuckin' faggot" will not move the air around my ears; and when my gay brother approaches me on the street that we can embrace if we choose.

I dare us to dream that we are worth wanting each other.

IV

Black men loving Black men is the revolutionary act of the eighties.

At eighteen, David could have been a dancer: legs grown strong from daily walks from his remote neighborhood to downtown in search of employment that would free him from his abusive family situation. David, soft-spoken and articulate, could have been a waiter gliding gracefully among the tables of a three-star restaurant. David could have performed numerous jobs, but lacking the connections that come with age and race, the Army seemed a reasonable choice. His grace and demeanor will be of little importance in Nicaragua.

Earl is always a good time. His appearance at parties, whether it's a smart cocktail sip or basement gig, is mandatory. He wakes with coffee and speed, enjoys three-joint lunches, and chases his bedtime Valium with Johnny Walker Red. None of his friends, of which he has many, suggest that he needs help. His substance abuse is ignored by all.

Stacy is a delirious queen, a concoction of current pop stars, bound eclectically in thrift store threads. His sharp and witty tongue can transform the most boring, listless evenings. In private, minus the dangles and bangles, he appears solemn and pensive, and speaks of the paucity of role models, mentors, and possibilities.

Maurice has a propensity for white people, which is more than preference—it's policy. He dismisses potential Black friendships as quickly as he switches off rap music and discredits progressive movements. He consistently votes Republican. At night he dreams of razors cutting away thin slivers of his Black skin.

Bubba and Ray had been lovers for so long that the neighbors presumed them to be brothers or widowers. For decades their socializing had been done among an intimate circle of gay couples, so when Ray died Bubba felt too old to venture the new gay scene. Occasionally he has visitors, an equally old friend or a much younger cousin or nephew. But mostly he sits, weather permitting, on the front porch where with a can of beer over ice, he silently weaves marvelous tales of "the life" in the thirties and forties. Yet there isn't anyone who listens.

Bobbi, a former drag queen, has plenty of time to write poetry. Gone are his makeup and high heels since he began serving his two-to-five year sentence. He had not wanted to kick that bouncer's ass; however, he, not unlike the more macho sissies clad in leather and denim, rightfully deserved admittance to that bar. Although he has had no visitors and just a couple of letters, he maintains a sense of humor typified by the title of a recent set of poems: *Where can a decent drag queen get a decent drink?*

Paul is hospitalized with AIDS. The severity of his illness is not known

94

Joseph Beam

to his family or friends. They cannot know that he is gay; it is his secret and he will expire with it. Living a lie is one thing, but it is quite another to die within its confines.

Charles is a ventman with beautiful dreads. On days when he is not drinking and is lucid, he will tell you how he winters on the south side of the square and sleeps facing the east so that he wakes with the sun in his eyes. He is only an obstacle to passersby.

Ty and Reggie have been lovers since they met in the service seven years ago. They both perform dull and menial jobs for spiteful employers, but plan to help each other through college. Ty will attend first. Their two-room apartment, which is neither fashionably appointed nor in a fashionable neighborhood, is clearly a respite from the madness that awaits outside their door. They would never imagine themselves as revolutionaries.

Black men loving Black men is the revolutionary act of the eighties, not only because sixties' revolutionaries like Bobby Seale, Huey Newton, and Eldridge Cleaver dare speak our name; but because as Black men we were never meant to be together—not as father and son, brother and brother—and certainly not as lovers.

Black men loving Black men is an autonomous agenda for the eighties, which is not rooted in any particular sexual, political, or class affiliation, but in our mutual survival. The ways in which we manifest that love are as myriad as the issues we must address. Unemployment, substance abuse, self-hatred, and the lack of positive images are but some of the barriers to our loving.

Black men loving Black men is a call to action, an acknowledgment of responsibility. We take care of our own kind when the night grows cold and silent. These days the nights are cold-blooded and the silence echoes with complicity.

Notes
1. Lorde, Audre. *The Cancer Journals.* Argyle, NY: Spinsters Ink, 1980.
2. Lorde, Audre. *Sister Outsider.* Ithaca, NY: Crossing Press, 1984.
3. Baldwin, James. *Village Voice,* Vol. 29, No. 26, p. 14.
4. Blackwomon, Julie. *Revolutionary Blues and Other Fevers.* Philadelphia: self-published, 1984. (Distributed by Kitchen Table: Women of Color Press, P.O. Box 908, Latham, New York.)

96

Diane DiMassa

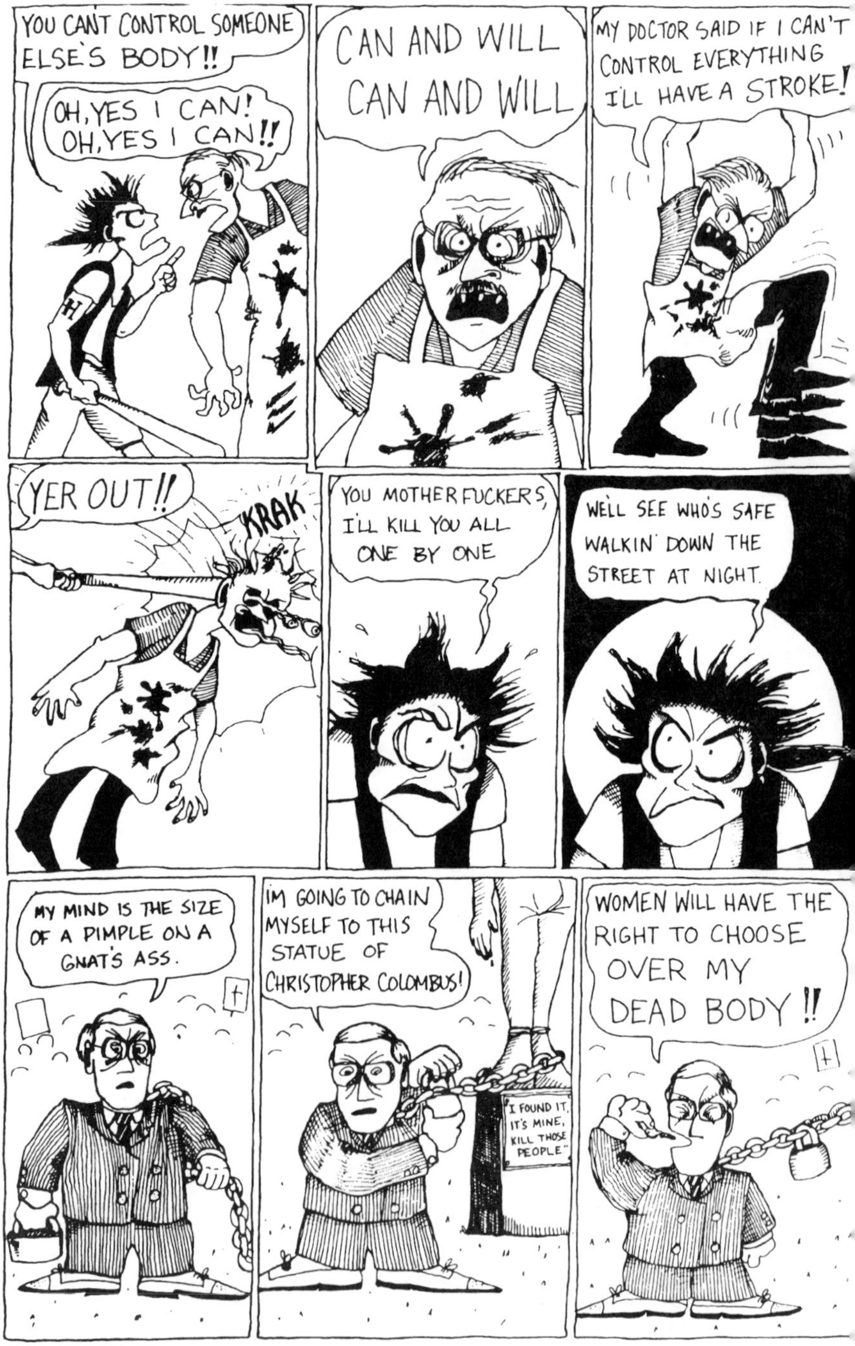

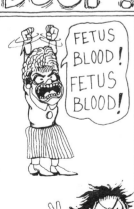

Diane
DiMassa

from "Gay Studies as Moral Vision"
from *Gay Ideas: Outing and Other Controversies*

R I C H A R D   D .   M O H R

In American Sign Language, the infinitive "to fuck" is indicated, not surprisingly, by the repeated passing of the index finger of one hand in and out of a hoop formed by the index finger and thumb of the other. One prepares to indicate a male orgasm by pursing and drawing palmward the fingertips of the right hand; then, one signs the infinitive "to cum" by poking the index finger of the left hand to the heel of the right, triggering its finger tips to thrust sharply away and somewhat apart. Another sign for a male climax is a blend of the signs for "gravy (drippings)" and "spread."

The signs for sexual activities in ASL are not mere abstract symbols, in the way, say, stars and stripes are symbols of America. Rather, they are pictographs, moving hieroglyphs. Unlike stars and stripes, which have reference by mere convention, the ASL expressions image and resemble the very things for which they serve as signs—vividly. In ASL, the signs for the following sexual or genital *acts* are also pictographs: "masturbation," "gay mutual masturbation," "vaginal masturbation," "cunnilingus," "fellatio," "gay male mutual oral sex," "anal intercourse," "group sex," and "rape." In its single concession to the existence of sexual discourse in ASL, the *American Sign Language Dictionary*, gives the same sign for the actions "copulate," "fornicate," and "sexual intercourse." It too is a pictograph: "(The motions of the legs during the sexual act.) The upturned left 'V' hand remains motionless, while the downturned right 'V' hand comes down repeatedly on the left."

However, the derogatory ASL expressions for gay men are not pictographs. Slang in ASL tends to be regional, but the most wide spread sign for "faggot" is the pinched tips of the index finger and thumb touched a couple of times to the chin. Another sign for "faggot" is the flitting of finger tips near the forward temple and corner of the eye, as though one were trying to cut and fluff the air there. A recent innovation for "faggot" is twice tugging an earlobe. Still another sign is the touching of the tip of the middle finger to the nose and then sweeping it up and over the crown of the head. An older sign is dry licking a fingertip with which one then quickly strokes the hairs of the corresponding eyebrow, as though one were painting them. ASL has shown considerably less "imagination" with lesbians. "Lesbian"—in all its connotations—is signed simply by holding the letter "L" to the chin. These expressions do not image actions. In particular, they do not image the acts that it might be argued place a person in the class of gay men. The signs simply presuppose that gay men as a class are worthy of derision independent of the acts that define an individual as a member of the class, and they contribute to the derision by enhancing stereotypes—of flightiness, misplaced femininity, and exaggeration. The gestural conventions of ASL clearly suggest that gay men are despised in virtue of some perceived group status that gays have rather than in virtue of the acts they perform.

Richard D. Mohr

The creation of slang is a nonreflective activity, and here, in ASL, slang unconsciously captures and conveys a basic truth about social attitudes toward gay men. Those who have reflected on the position of gays in modern social structures have shown a marked tendency to misunderstand this truth. In his seminal work of the early 1960s *Stigma,* Erving Goffman advances the following cosmology of the dispossessed:

> Three grossly different types of stigma may be mentioned. First there are abominations of the body—the various physical deformities. Next there are blemishes of individual character perceived as weak will, domineering or unnatural passions, treacherous and rigid beliefs, and dishonesty, these being *inferred from a known record of,* for example, mental disorder, imprisonment, addiction, alcoholism, *homosexuality,* unemployment, suicidal attempts, and radical political behavior. Finally there are the tribal stigmas of race, nation and religion, these being stigmas that can be transmitted through lineages and equally contaminate all members of the family.

This cosmology, which categorizes homosexuals by what they do, or allegedly do, has proved amazingly persistent in liberal American thought. It is even imaged in the American Civil Liberties Union's current basic brochure *Guardian of Freedom:* "ACLU programs…have most often been on behalf of people with the special vulnerability of the powerless: members of racial and ethnic minorities; women; children; those subjected to the arbitrary discipline of closed institutions such as mental patients, prisoners and servicemen; the poor; non-conformists of every kind, from splinter radical parties to gays to anti-war protesters."

These quotes presume that *in society's eyes* gays are essentially performers of radical acts akin to those of political activists. This presumption could not be farther from the truth. The record of those social forms in which stigma and derision are most clearly advanced against groups—slang, jokes, stereotypes, violence, symbolic legislation, and judicial abuse—shows what ASL shows, namely, that society does not treat gays as of a piece with radical politicians, social misfits, alcoholics, suicides, and the like, who are grouped by acts that they perform. Neither is homosexuality chiefly viewed as a flaw of individual character (like being nasty or rude). And it certainly is not viewed as a character inferred from a known record of behavior. It is not by their behavior that gays are judged and classified. Rather, the evidence in lopsided preponderance shows that society ranks homosexuals with racial groups and the physically deformed. Stigmas against gays are a blend of Goffman's abominations of the flesh and tribal stigmas. Gays are viewed first and foremost simply as morally lesser beings, like animals, children, or dirt, *not* as failed full moral agents. Objections of some religions and conservatives to the contrary, it is against the sinner, not the sin, that society deploys the armaments of anti-gay oppression. Such acts as gays are thought to perform—whether sexual, gestural, or social—are viewed socially as the expected or even necessary efflorescence of gays' lesser moral state, of their status as lesser beings, rather than as the distinguishing marks by which they are defined as a group. Such purported acts—the stuff of stereotypes—provide the materials for a retrospectively constructed ideology concocted to justify the group's despised status, in the way, for instance, that the social belief that Jews, Germans, Japanese, or Native Americans poison wells is concocted, as socially "needed," to justify society's hatred of these groups. Here, hatred's fixing of status is primitive and behavior an ideologically inspired afterthought.

…[S]uch moral classification of gays by status rather than action is at work in major legal forms—immigration policy, marital law, the military, the Supreme Court, and lesser courts. In the mid-1980s, two other major institutions weighed in to this classificatory model—religion and medicine. In 1986, the Catholic church, in a major ideological shift, branded as "an objective moral disorder" the mere status of being a homosexual, even when congenitally fixed and unaccompanied by any homosexual behavior. Previously, such status had been held morally neutral, and only homosexual acts were morally censured. This retooled racism, although new in the church's treatment of gays, simply codifies what society has believed all along anyway; here, the church's barbarism is simply trying to catch up with the times.

103

from "Gay Studies as Moral Vision"

**Richard D.
Mohr**

On April 15, 1985, in Atlanta during her keynote address for the First International Conference on AIDS, President Reagan's cabinet secretary of health and human services, Margaret Heckler, in a burst of good intentions gone painfully awry, held: "We must conquer AIDS before it affects the heterosexual population…the general population. We have a very strong public interest in stopping AIDS before it spreads outside the risk groups, before it becomes an overwhelming problem." The determinate prospect of a million or so dead gay men was not seen to be a problem for the Reagan administration. Now, in America, we do not normally distinguish the worth of individual lives with respect to the means by which people come to have diseases. We do not, for instance, think that the life of a CEO who suffers a heart attack from years of gluttony is worth less than a person who suffers a heart attack under torture. Even if one drew a moral distinction between the AIDS-conveying sex acts of heterosexuals and those of homosexuals, this would still not ground a further distinction between lives to be saved and lives to be junked. So it is not the moral assessment of actions that grounds Heckler's distinction; rather, she holds heterosexual status as more worthy of care and concern than gay status. Gays, here, are lesser beings.

The social understanding of homosexuality as essentially a degenerate status rather than a form of behavior has important consequences for understanding gay men and lesbians as a minority and for understanding the objects and objectives of lesbian and gay studies. In its most central, frequent, and important usage, "minority" is a normative rather than a descriptive term. Its use in its descriptive, statistical meaning—"less than 50 percent"—is rare (one example can be found in the sentence "Ontario's Progressive Conservatives after forty years of continuous rule are now a minority party in the Ontario parliament"). The more common, normative rather than statistical sense of the term was clearly evinced in media discussions over where AIDS was going in the late 1980s. Once it appeared that Margaret Heckler's prediction was incorrect, that white heterosexual males were not coming down with AIDS in great numbers, the media needed to find some other place on which to settle its concern for the disease and settled on "minorities." But not once in this media blitz were gay men named a "minority." Indeed, the term was regularly used in ways that necessarily implied that gays were not a "minority" affected by AIDS, even though a constitutional majority of AIDS cases were falling on that but five or so percent of the population that is gay and male.

Now, "minority," is a concept that is both norm dependent and norm invoking: that is, on the one hand, for the correct application of "minority," certain normative conditions must be fulfilled, and in turn, on the other hand, once correctly applied, "minority" prescribes certain norms, calls for certain actions. Perhaps surprisingly, in its norm-dependent dimension, "minority" seems not to entail any nonmoral facts. At least it does not entail the term's descriptive or statistical sense. The expression now found in job advertisements encouraging "women and other minorities to apply" shows that the statistical sense of "minority" is not a necessary condition for the correct application of the term taken in its normative sense. To the chagrin of some black leaders, minority set-aside programs for federal contracts count the statistical majority *women* as a minority.

On what, then, does "being a minority" turn? I think American Sign Language, the Catholic church, and Margaret Heckler provide sufficient clues. A minority is a group treated unjustly because of some status that the group is socially perceived to possess independently of the behavior of the group's members. This definition captures the scope and normative force of the term. On it, women, although statistically a majority, are a minority, but the statistical minority people-with-blue-eyes is not. Not surprisingly, there are no minority set-aside programs in federal contracts for people with blue eyes. Yet, given this definition, current discussions of gays as a minority have been largely misguided because irrelevant.

Almost all the popular debate about gays—and a fair amount of the academic—has turned on whether being gay is an immutable characteristic. If it is, gays would be, so it is claimed, relevantly like blacks—like in that one's group characteristic is not of one's own doing, with the result that in a group-based discrimination one is treated unjustly because treated without regard to what one oneself has done. But even if it were conclusively proved that being gay is not a matter of choice, such a biology-based or psychology-based strategy gets morality on the cheap, indeed too cheaply.

Sometimes, drawing moral distinctions with respect to nonchosen properties is morally acceptable, even morally to be expected. For example, "grandfather provisions" are not, on their own, considered unjust. A law with a grandfather provision blocks future access to a privilege but allows those currently with the privilege to maintain it (say, a vendor's license or a past land use in the face of newly restrictive zoning). If grandfather exceptions do not front for some illegitimate goal (e.g., perpetuating racial oppression in the post-Reconstruction era), then they are not felt to be substantially unjust, even though they create closed classes of people with privileges to which others, sometimes as a matter of when they were born, can have no access no matter what they do. Or again, a law that lowers the inheritance tax rate will disadvantage a person whose parents have already died compared to people whose parents have not yet died. Still, this disadvantage is not an injustice to him even though its falling on him is not a consequence of anything that he has done.

from "Gay
Studies
as Moral
Vision"

**Richard D.
Mohr**

When taken as a moral principle, the claim that one is not to be discriminated against with respect to some property over which one has no control has all the usefulness but roughness of a rule of thumb—immutable characteristics *usually* will be morally irrelevant. Yet if we suppose that good reasons ought to stand behind all claims of morality and immorality, then the principle does not produce even a presumption, let alone trumping judgment, of immorality for exceptions to it since the exceptions themselves will have good reasons standing behind them. A more accurate principle is the broader, if blander, one that a person is not to be treated in ways that are irrelevant to the person's immutable properties or that a person's immutable properties are not to be given a moral weight that they do not warrant. And the relevant principle of social equality, then, is not the clean, clear one holding that distinctions may not be drawn with respect to people's immutable characteristics, but the more sinuous principle holding that people may not be held in lesser moral regard irrespective of what they have done. Distinctions may be drawn without reference to individuals' moral responsibility, but when such distinctions are drawn, they must not degrade those individuals. For instance, if it were established that exclusive homosexuality is an immutable characteristic, that finding would not instantly make baby bonuses a violation of rights to equal protection because of the favorable disparate impact and economies of scale that such bonuses would have for heterosexual households. Whether they were to be barred would depend on whether the policy enhanced social structures that degraded gays. And to determine that would require looking at social customs. Sometimes, fixed physical characteristics are morally relevant.

Yet immutable characteristics are not necessary conditions for moral minority status. Among star cases of minorities that have properly invoked civil and constitutional protections are religious minorities and the physically challenged—and the physically challenged even when the challenge in question is the result of personal responsibility as in a negligently caused car accident or a botched suicide. Those who take skin color as the exclusive paradigm for minority status, then, are simply ignorant of actual social circumstance and current justified law. Minority standing that is based on biological or psychological determinism lets in both too much and too little.

Determinists miss the moral dimension of minority status in another major way as well. The sources of injustice against groups lie chiefly in the nature of society's treatment of the group rather than in the selection of any objective characteristics of the group on which the treatment focuses. Injustice against minorities lies chiefly in the *manner* or *mode* of social operations rather than in the operations being directed at the wrong *objects*. Consider slavery. Slavery is not a social treatment the remedy for which might be found in a shift in its focus, say, from blacks to blondes. Or again, slavery would not become an acceptable way to treat blacks if some alchemist's alembic produced an inexpensive pill that could convert to white both primary and secondary Negroid features, such that being black became a mutable characteristic.

No, the injustice of slavery is not that it has the wrong objects. Nor is the source of its injustice that it causes unwarranted unhappiness, nor even that, like a tax too high, it unjustifiably restricts independence. Rather the injustice of slavery in virtue of which its direction at blacks established blacks as a normative minority is that it views blacks as lesser moral beings. Whatever may be said of the Supreme Court's subsequent race cases, it correctly understood the moral dynamics of slavery when in 1857 it held that blacks could not be considered U.S. citizens by the founding fathers because, as the Court wrote, "that unfortunate race...[was correctly] regarded as being of an inferior order, and altogether unfit to associate with the white race, either in social or political relations; and so far inferior, that they had no rights which the white man was bound to respect; and that the negro might justly and lawfully be reduced to slavery for his own benefit."

An alarming number of current-day racist jokes continue this same moral vision—that blacks are not moral agents but lesser beings that exist (or even perish) for the sake of use in the projects of "fully" human beings: "How many blacks does it take to shingle a roof? Just two if you slice them thin enough." It is only as signaling lesser moral standing rather than failed moral agency that race is relevant here. Any treatment of other groups that puts them in the same moral orbit, that of lesser moral status rather than failed moral agency, would equally justify the application to them of the moral sense of "minority" and in turn invoke the civil and constitutional norms we think appropriate for minority status. Society's treatment of gays—as shown in its treatment of them in slang and invective, derogatory group-based jokes, stereotypes, group-directed violence, symbolic legislation, and, as we have seen, Catholic theology, health policy, and constitutional law—does exactly this: presuppose and reinforce the moral vision that gays are lesser moral beings. Whether gays are or are not in fact objectively like a highly distinctive ethnic group, that is how society views and treats them—as a despised ethnic minority and not as a pack of criminals. It is this, rather than because sexual orientation is or is viewed as some immutable characteristic or social statistic, that makes gays a minority.

To summarize, even if the biological determinists are right about their facts, they are, in the main, irrelevant in establishing gays as a minority.

Now, my thesis that society treats gays *as though* they constitute an ethnic minority does not entail and should not be confused with a some-

from "Gay Studies as Moral Vision"

what different claim about the relation between nature, culture, and sexuality. I am not claiming that, either in its general arrangements or in its specific treatment of gays, society constitutes or constructs homosexuality (whether behavioral, gestural, or social) *as a sexual category*. The social constructionist claims that social forces do not simply shape the direction or expression of homosexuality, understood as a presocietal natural kind, but enter into its very definition, such that social structures, especially structures of discourse, rather than natural properties, establish gays as a sexual minority. For them, "gayness"—and note the shift to the abstract noun—is now understood intentionally, not extensionally, that is, is understood as a "meaning" or classificatory matrix of concepts rather than as—and independently of—any actual designatable group of persons in the world. Here, "minority" is understood as a small category—small simply because but one of various and sundry such categories. The social constructionists' position, even if true, is as irrelevant to the normative sense of minorities as is the view of their opponents, the biological determinists. Their irrelevance intriguingly mirrors the materialists'. They can offer explanations, but not justifications; they can offer facts, but not values. Indeed, their relativism—"one person says one thing, another another; one culture says one thing, another another"—ought to make them skeptical that any critical morality is possible.

The role of nonmoral facts in morality is that they set the limit of the morally possible. Perhaps this fact about facts explains paradoxically why the early great works that one is most tempted to call gay studies, works chiefly of history and anthropology, have *appeared* to have such a strong moral component. Their great virtue has not been explanation but revelation. Who would have thought that such stuff was out there—in past Christianity, in New Guinea, among Native American peoples? Who would have thought that there were so many possibilities? The limits of the possible have been dilated hugely, while that which previously appeared good because seemingly necessary and natural is now seen to be just one more damn thing. But we must not read positive moral claims into these findings. To change the horizon is not to set a course. What might be done does not tell us what ought to be done.

My model of gay studies, then, views gay studies as the study of a minority but offers an understanding of "minority" that is a tertium quid. Minority status is a moral vision, and gay studies, as the study of a minority, should be viewed chiefly as a normative inquiry rather than as either an empirical study of the world or a nonempirical study of discourses. The normative object of any minority study—and the chief reason that one is properly motivated to bother with the study in the first place—is the social treatment of a group that is socially defined independently of the behavior

Richard D. Mohr

of its members. The form and end of gay studies is the evaluation of the treatment of gays so viewed and, in turn, the prescription of social forms in light of that moral evaluation. The architectonic of gay studies is not knowledge in the sense of the accumulation and systematizing of empirical facts and the hypothesizing of causal relations among them those facts. On the one hand, then, gay studies is not paramountly concerned with the biological or psychological features of the group's members. On the other hand, the relevant social treatment of the group—its moral treatment—is not to be confused with the alleged social construction of the minority as a category into which individuals might fall through either social forces or self-definition. Gay studies ought not to devolve into either biology or social history, as it currently seems to be doing. We have been playing things safe, perhaps too safe. History, anthropology, sociology, and literary studies make gays appear acceptable and nonthreatening because muted and transmuted by tales of the past, the exotics of distance, the abstractions of statistics, or the irrelevance of theory's jargon. We need to be a bit braver and say that gay studies matters because gay people matter—here, now, and breathing.

from "Gay
Studies
as Moral
Vision"

from "The Surprise Party"
from *Macho Sluts*

PAT CALIFIA

She had short hair and never wore anything but Levis, boots, a black or white T-shirt, and a leather jacket. Every time she went out the door, she squared her shoulders, straightened her spine, and put purpose in her walk. When the way you look makes it clear that you are a queer sort of queer, each unmolested step down the street is a victory. Live defensively, she told herself as she strained to extend her peripheral vision to shield her sides and back. Sometimes she concentrated so hard on not smiling, not moving her ass from side to side, not giving any sign of vulnerability, that she stopped thinking for several minutes about nights when cars had screamed to a stop, disgorging gangs that chanted insults as they ran, and stopped scanning litter baskets for bottles she could break, just in case.

It was twilight. She was trying to keep her footing, going down a very steep hill. A cop car purred up the street. Everybody who sees a black-and-white feels a tiny spurt of adrenaline hit their system. The anxiety and the extra energy don't go away until you know for sure they aren't looking for you. Relax, she admonished herself. They're just on patrol. No sirens, no flashing lights, relax, relax.

Brakes screeched. Doors flew open. Feet hit the pavement. And hands reached out of the dark, took her from behind by both elbows, and propelled her through the soft night air to the cold metal side of the car. Their grip on her was professional—tight enough to express their muscle, but not hard enough to bruise. She caught glimpses of uniforms, truncheons, pistol hilts, shiny visors, handcuffs, badges, hairy wrists wearing heavy silver watches.

There were three of them, two city cops and one in a highway patrol uniform. "What is he doing here with them?" she thought, and then the rage came up and made her skin white-hot and her stomach cold and sick. The pig who was holding her felt the rising threat build in her frame, and he used her arm to twist her up onto her toes, then slapped cuffs on her wrists.

"Go ahead," he said softly in a good-ole-boy drawl, "resist arrest. I'd love it." He had blond hair and a slightly red, mean cracker face. His navy blue, wool-covered groin brushed briefly against her hip, then he withdrew, kicked her feet wide apart, and held her against the car with his truncheon pointed into the small of her back.

The whole thing had taken no time at all, and she was helpless and hating them and afraid. Why was this happening? Oh, God, God, God, I have the right to remain silent, who will I call, oh, God, *this* can't be happening.

* * *

Joe and Mike were standing hip to hip, their hands on each other's flies. Light glinted off their nightsticks and the textured plastic grips of their revolvers. The sight of men handling each other was a sure-fire turn-on, despite her abraded face and Don's bigoted remarks. What a kinky little triad she had stumbled onto! The highway patrolman was behind her, buckling the soft leather hospital restraints around her upper arms. He fastened them very close together, pulling her shoulders back and making her breasts arch out. He stood behind her, holding her head, making her watch the two policemen fondle each other. Finally, they unzipped and began to rub and slap their exposed hard-ons together. When Don snapped his fingers, each of them removed a Trojan from his uniform shirt pocket and rolled it over his buddy's dick.

"Good boys. This is where you come in," he said, and shoved her toward them. She inched forward on her knees, and each of them reached out a hand to bring her into their circle. It was a blissful interlude. They competed with each other to slip into her mouth. While she sucked one, hot and deep, the other would rub his cock against her cheeks and neck, or press it into his partner's hand, or stroke it himself. At one point, she was feasting alternately on their balls. She had to bend her head way back to get to them, and while the furry sacs filled her cheeks, their erections rested along her nose and forehead, leaving little wet saliva marks under her hairline. One of them even rubbed his cock all over her crewcut, gasping at the feel of the short hair tickling his prick. They tried to make her suck both cocks at the same time, and she briefly succeeded in getting two heads into her mouth, but she could not keep her teeth out of the way, so they alternated, six strokes apiece, moving her from shaft to shaft. She spluttered, drooled, choked, and dived after them.

Joe's dick was shorter and thicker, with a somewhat flat head—a piledriver. Mike's was proportioned more like a mushroom, the cap much bigger than the long, slender stem.

from "The Surprise Party"

"I'm gonna come, Don," Joe began to pant. "I mean sir, sir, shall I come in her mouth or what? Tell me quick, please! Huh-huh-huh!"

"Unload," Don told him, smoking his cigar.

This time she didn't have any trouble keeping his whole dick down without choking while he came. The extra-thick shape was no problem without the length that triggered her gag reflex. Joe pulled out, one hand wrapped around the base of his now-flaccid meat to hold the loose rubber on. She didn't see what he did with it because Don spoke suddenly, sardonically, and instantly had her full attention.

"What about you, Mike? Gonna get your rocks off any time soon?"

Mike's erection faltered. She moved to take him deeper, protectively, in her mouth, to hide the evidence of his softened cock from his master. "Not just yet," he said, tickling her ears.

"I know you," the tall patrolman said. "You can't come without a little extra attention, can you, mister?"

"No, sir, I can't, sir."

The patrolman moved behind him and took him in his arms. The black-gloved hands unbuttoned his shirt and began to play with his flat nipples, barely visible in the mat of chest hair. Suddenly, she had more cock than she could handle. Mike gripped her to him, refusing to let her get away, and pumped into her throat. The harder Don worked his tits, the harder he got and the deeper he thrust into her soft tissues. She felt like an Accujac, a convenient sex toy being used to help these two men get off with each other. Mike had only one hand on her head now, and she could see that the other one was behind him, busily working Don up to full erection.

Now Don's hands were on Mike's cock, and he was jerking him off, slowly and insistently milking his rosy shaft. "I'm going to jerk him off in your mouth," he told her coldly. "Isn't that exciting? Pinch your own tits, Mike, I want you to fill up that scumbag with fresh spunk. You better produce a lot of cream, boy, or it's your ass. You, cocksucker, don't take that rubber off him until I can see the size of his load."

They continued that way—Mike pulling on his own tits, Don pumping his cock, her twirling her tongue around the head of Mike's dick—until he came, copiously, and sagged, weak in the knees. "God, it's hard to come standing up," he complained.

Don let go of him, grabbed the prophylactic and slid it off. "You forgot to say thank you," he grinned. "Now git down on the floor next to her." Mike hesitated, and his face turned red. Don shouted, "I said kneel, you punk!"

Mike obeyed him with bad grace, giving her one furious glance that wiped the smile off her face. Don took Mike's face in his big hand and forced his mouth open. "Swallow it," Don said, squeezing the contents of the used rubber onto his tongue. He did, grimacing. She could only imag-

112

Pat Califia

ine how your own cum would taste, cold. Don's hard-on was in her face, and she transferred her attention to it. Mike mumbled, "Thank you, sir," with obvious lack of sincerity, and got to his own feet while Don reached down for her and helped her up.

He turned her and held her the way he had held Mike. His leather-clad hands felt her breasts, dug briefly into her sore armpits, then reached for her belt buckle and undid it and the top button of her jeans. One hand slid inside her pants, the other hand undoing buttons until he could cup his fingers around her cunt. The heel of his palm rested against her clit, and his long fingers dabbled in her juices, then pierced her hole and filled it. "I'm sorry to see you're all dry and reluctant," he said, biting her ear. "Joe, Mike!" He indicated her boots. The two came over and lifted her feet one at a time, removed her boots and socks, then tugged her jeans down over her hips. All her clothes were piled with the jacket on the dusty armchair.

He was so tall, he had to pull her off her feet to get his hand around her cunt. His jacket creaked, smelling deliciously of leather and armpits. He began to chew her neck and shoulder, his fingers moving just enough to make her cunt feel good. His hard cock pressed against her buttocks, smearing thick liquid into her crack. Did his cock just leak continually, she wondered, constantly secreting this stream of sex juice?

"You lied to me before," he said, flicking one of her nipples. "Remember? You told me you didn't like it. But you do. I'm your worst fear and your best fantasy. You're just pissed because I haven't fucked you yet." He went to work on the other side of her throat. His moustache burned, his mouth sucked and licked her, his teeth left puncture marks and bite marks from her ear down her neck all the way across her shoulder. Her hands were pressed against his pubic hair, and she had just enough mobility in the hospital restraints to be able to fondle his balls. When he felt her touch, he bit her harder and dug his fingers deeper into her vagina. Finally, he lifted his head. "Joe, clean her out, okay?"

Joe approached her, swinging a guard-dog training collar in one hand. Each of its chain links were attached to prongs which would lay flat when the dog's leash had slack in it. If the dog lunged, the leash would pull the prongs up and make them dig into the dog's neck. Naked, collared, and with arms bound behind her, she was easy to control. He led her into the bathroom. A douche hose dangled from the shower head, and this familiar sight was so incongruous, she erupted into helpless laughter. Joe grinned, then turned his back on her to hide his expression, twirled the faucets, and tested the temperature of the water flowing through the hose. Mike joined them, sat on the toilet, bent her over his knee and greased her ass, then held her there, keeping the tips of his fingers just barely inside it. She could feel the calluses on his hands.

from "The Surprise Party"

"How far up should we clean?" Joe asked, spurting hose in hand. He could have been an obscene statue in a garden fountain. She barely repressed a hysterical giggle.

Don was watching them from the doorway. He had retrieved and relit his cigar. "I don't know. Hey, bitch-dog. You. Dyke. Ever had a fist up your ass?"

"Never!"

"Not yet, anyway. How about a cock?"

There was a long silence.

"Well, well, well. I guess I'm never going to get to fuck me a virgin. How many, fur-pie? *Answer me!*"

"A few."

114

Pat Califia

"Meaning you don't remember. Well, Joe, I'd say you ought to clean it up to the second sphincter. Mike's kind of fastidious, and I wouldn't want him to get any caca on his pretty long schlong. But I don't think you have to give her a high colonic. We haven't got all week."

While this diagnosis was being made, Joe had maneuvered her into the tiled cubicle, and her bowel had been filling with warm water. He removed the hose, and she yipped with alarm as a small trickle of water escaped along with it. She cried out again as Don's belt swung overhead and landed right on her ass. "No spills," he warned her. "You don't get rid of that until I say so. Now crawl over here and lick my big, fascist boots. Come on, put your ass up in the air and pray over 'em." The belt landed again and again, but she somehow maintained her control and kept the dreadful weight of water bottled up inside her guts. His boot-leather was smooth and tasted of fine polish. God, it was good to grovel on the floor and savor them. He didn't let her up until her ass was bright red and both boots were shiny with her spit.

They perched her on the toilet and stood close, cocks out, helping each other into condoms, while torrents of water rushed out of her ass. "God, you stink," Don growled, and shoved his dick into her mouth. They fucked her face while she shat again and again, and kept fucking her mouth long after the cramps had subsided. Then the process was repeated—more water, a tongue-bath for Joe's and Mike's shoes, another session on the throne and choking on their sheathed dicks, one after another, as fast as they could pull her mouth down onto one, off of it, and onto another. Would she ever be able to close her mouth and swallow again?

Finally, when her insides had been pronounced squeaky-clean, they removed the hospital restraints and collar and shoved her under the shower. While two of them guarded her under the water, one would disrobe. Joe and Mike put on jockstraps, police boots, and their gun belts. Don removed his shirt and trousers, then replaced his Sam Browne belt and boots. His jock was made out of studded leather. He kept the belt he had removed earlier from his motorcycle jacket in his hand. Watching this transformation, she shuddered with lust, turning in the hot water, wishing there were some way to avoid this confrontation with her fantasies, and deeply glad that there was no escape.

Their nearly-naked bodies were alien to her. Their hips were too flat, shoulders too broad, nipples too small and flat, their muscles came in long plates, and they were covered with fur everywhere. Don's auburn fuzz contrasted pleasantly with Mike's blond, almost invisible hair and Joe's abundant black bear fur. Their asses were square, narrow. They even smelled strange—had a tang about them that women did not.

The water was turned off, Joe and Mike grabbed her, and under Don's orders they carried her over to the bed. She was still dripping wet, so they rolled her back and forth on the sheet, then both of them began to lick her, removing the moisture from her skin with their tongues. Almost shyly, their mouths covered her breasts and sucked up her nipples, their tongues strayed into her armpit and down her sides, penetrated her mouth and caressed her thighs.

"How does she taste?" Don demanded. "You two queer bastards ever done anything like this with a girl before?"

They both denied it.

"Well, dive in, assholes. Lick her everywhere. I'd love to see your queer faces buried in that snatch but I'm afraid y'all might acquire a taste for it. So you just use your fingers, you hear? And keep 'em on the outside. No finger-banging. Just juice her up. It's a pity, 'cause you boys could really learn how to muff-dive from our friend here. I bet she knows how to suck pussy real good, don't you, sweetheart?"

She admitted it, barely coherent, driven out of her mind by the tongues lapping all over her body and the fingers that spread lubrication up and down, again and again, from her clit to her asshole, but kept her empty, driving her to produce more and more fluid. She could feel the shape of her own internal sex-parts, knew how deep her vagina went and the angle it took, by the way it ached to be pushed open and stroked. But she was not allowed to direct or guide what was happening in any way. Joe continued to tongue and massage her, but Mike let her hands go long enough to remove his jock. When he returned, his balls drooped in her face.

"Swallow his nuts," Don ordered her. "I see you trying to lick his balls. You—stuff 'em in her mouth. Sit on her face."

Mike, still angry about having been ordered to the floor beside her, was only too happy to oblige. Disregarding his own comfort, he crammed his entire ballsac into her mouth. She retaliated by sucking hard on his eggs, then clamping her lips tightly around them, and running her tongue and her teeth across the taut skin of his scrotum. He must not have minded too

from "The
Surprise
Party"

much because he pulled away from her enough to stretch his sac even more, and began to play with himself, dripping sweat and pre-cum onto her breasts.

Joe was lying on his stomach between her legs, his fingers busy, licking her thighs. She could tell that he really wanted to go ahead and put his tongue there, in that forbidden groove, but was afraid of Don's wrath. Nevertheless, he was slipping a finger or two into her occasionally, despite the strict prohibition against this misbehavior. Her lips swelled, parted, and became incredibly slippery. When Don spoke, they both jumped.

"You like the way that smells?" Don sneered. Joe didn't even turn around. "It smells like sex, sir," he said softly.

Don ignored that response and ordered his subordinates to jack off just enough to keep their dicks hard. "I want to be able to look over there and see you enjoying yourselves," he said.

Pat Califia

Then Joe began to really get the idea of how a clit worked and started to do something that felt like it would make her come, if only it didn't change or stop. He had the tip of his little finger resting at her ass, the pad of his middle finger resting over the opening of her vagina, and held her clit between his thumb and index finger, barely moving it inside the hood. She lost track of what she was doing with her mouth. Mike lifted his ass to prevent his balls from getting mauled and pinned her hands down hard. God, that made it feel even better! Joe's fingers worked like some secret passion, and her cunt opened up like a wanton flower. He was resting his face on her thigh, and his beard scraped her delicate skin, inflaming it. She began to cry and toss on the bed.

"Don't make her come!" Don said sharply. What a completely hateful man. "I don't want her to come unless she's got something up one of her holes. You boys ever fucked any snatch?"

Mike drawled, "Oh, yeah, a time or two. I prefer BJs to busting cherries, myself." Why did she have a feeling that he was lying?

"Once. It wasn't a hell of a lot of fun," Joe said. "By the time I got it in I was so hot from carrying on and fighting about it that I came on her leg. She was pretty pissed about that."

"Well, you're going to fuck one now. This one. Both of you. I don't want any excuses, and I don't want any piss-poor performances. This isn't the back seat of your daddy's car, and you ain't in high school any more. Maybe it will help if you don't think of her as a girl. After all, she doesn't want to be a woman. She wants to be a man. She dresses like one, talks like one, walks like one. She's a queer, like you boys. Queers have sex with other queers, right? So who wants to go first?"

Joe, already kneeling between her legs, said, "Yo, sir. I sure would like to fuck her butt."

"I don't give a shit what you want. You can stick it in the hole I give you, or you can beat off in the corner. Mike, hold her down real good."

Joe hauled her closer to the foot of the bed. He bent her legs until her feet were in the air, then began to rub his hard cock over her wet, crumpled inner lips. For a few minutes, he fucked the outside of her pussy, where the swollen outer lips made a nice, snug channel for him. After awhile, she understood that he was teasing her, and that he wanted her to struggle to get his cock. Well, why not? She had never felt emptier. Her beaten ass was burning, urging her on. "Please," she moaned, writhing under him. "Please put it in me."

"You sure?" he teased, taking another condom from Don.

"Yes! Yes! Yes!"

"Come and get it," he grunted, hunching his hips. His dick head stroked her clit.

Pinned under him, she had almost no mobility, but she made whatever motions with her hips she could, trying to find his cock and impale herself on it. Meanwhile, Mike was holding down her hands, and she knew from the beads of sex juice that kept falling on her cheeks and forehead that he was enjoying what he saw. Don said, "We better slow you down, mister," and shoved a skin into his hand. Once again, Mike gave her an evil look of resentment. I wonder if he just hates me because I get to be the bottom, she thought. But there was too much good stuff going on below her waist to worry about the sulky redneck who was getting a fresh (and numbing) grip on her wrists after taking the pause that protects.

"You want it?" Joe demanded. "Here, feel how big it is." He thrust the head of his thick cock against her hole, not inserting it, but stretching the membrane taut. "It's going to fill you right up. Sure you can take it? Huh?"

"Yesssssss!"

An inch at a time, he teased her sheath down over his head and shaft. He was right—she felt stretched wide open. And then he began to move! Her eyes rolled back in her head, Mike started jabbing his cockhead between her lips, and her tongue flickered out to service him. Her head was turned sideways to accommodate him, and even shallow penetration put tremendous strain on her neck and shoulders. She sucked him as long as she could before Joe's pounding hips became too insistent and she again lost control over her mouth. "I'm afraid I'm going to bite you," she mumbled, and he hastened to pull out.

Her own experience with straight sex had been as unsatisfying as Mike's and Joe's. But this act of penetration was firmly situated within a context of dominance and submission—the core of her eroticism. She had been brought to a point where there was nothing she craved more. There could be no self-deception, no lies about not really wanting it. And these

from "The
Surprise
Party"

men were incredibly good at what they did. They liked fucking and being fucked, they knew how to do it, and they wanted her to like it. The element of mutual homosexuality made it seem more perverse, yet safe.

Joe churned inside her, speeding his rhythm. She tried to spread her legs wider, to open her hole up more, but he kept them clamped down, apparently preferring to fuck her tight, to feel the maximum resistance to his bulk. "Do you want it?" he panted. "Do you want me to come?"

"Yes!" she snarled, and worked with him to make it happen. He pushed especially deep inside her, jabbed her sharp and fast, his hands dug painfully into her ass cheeks, his thigh muscles went rigid. She could swear she actually felt the bulb of his dickhead swell, and knew by his convulsive hip movements that he had come.

"Very nice," Don said sarcastically. Oh, God. He had seen everything. She flushed and tried to hide her face against Mike's thigh. He shook her off, refusing to help. Joe had disappeared, probably gone off to take a leak, and Don was probing between her legs . "Did you come?" he asked her, leather-clad fingers moving where Joe had been.

Pat Califia

"I don't think I care about coming any more," she said, evasively but quite truthfully. "It all feels so good I don't want to come. I'm just afraid it will stop."

"Stop?" His head jerked erect. "We're just getting started. Number two!" He snapped his fingers, and Mike released her hands.

"Sir," Mike said, "Can I tie this bitch up and put some clamps on her tits?"

Don thought about it. "I don't see why not. It'll make it more fun to watch. But if you don't throw a really good fuck into her after that, I'm going to be real disappointed in you."

Mike froze at the menace in his master's voice. "No, you won't be disappointed, sir," he said. "I really want to fuck this cunt until she screams. Something about her just brings it out in me. But I need to have her hurt while I'm doing it. And I need to have her tied up so she can't get away. You want her to come, don't you? Well, I suspect that'll make her come real good."

"Oh? Yeah, you're probably right. She's just a slut, but she's a masochistic slut. Fix her the way you want her."

She was too tired to fight. Mike rolled her onto her stomach and slapped leather restraints on each wrist, then manacled her hands to the iron rails at the head of the bed. He also fastened restraints around each ankle, had her draw her legs up until she was kneeling, then fastened them at the sides of the bed. Then he reached under her and clamped her nipples into gleaming silver jaws. If she didn't keep her ass up in the air and her shoulders arched, she would be lying on the clamps.

He knelt behind her and ran his hands over her body once, twice. Then he used his nails. She twisted, but could not get away from him or close her legs. Every time she moved, she brought her slippery, vulnerable folds into contact with his jutting cock. He leaned over her and played with her tits, sending jolts of pain through her nipples, made her tell him how much it hurt and how wet it made her cunt. He slapped her ass with the flat of his hand until it began to glow and burn again. His hand fell with more and more weight. Bottoms, she thought, are so much meaner than tops. They have no sense of pacing. She screamed as much because he was making her angry as because it hurt a lot, but she doubted that he cared why as long as he knew he was hurting her.

Unlike Joe, he went into her in one vicious thrust, and she screamed. Tears sprang into her eyes. His long, skinny cock was stretching her in a very different way. It was much easier for her cunt to open wider than it was for it to become deeper. He was not waiting for her to open up, and she would be damned if she would ask him.

She did not want to come with him. Her vagina was a little sore, but his attitude bothered her more. Joe was an earthy little bull who could probably fuck anything that walked, but this southern redneck was in her only because Don told him to do it, and he was determined to make her pay for the humiliation Don had inflicted upon him in front of her. Nevertheless, when he reached underneath her and began to fondle her clitoris while his penis moved in and out of her hole, she almost started to spasm. Her sexual flesh was so congested that what happened to it mattered a great deal more than what went on in her head.

Don, that bastard, noticed, and moved in closer to watch. "You almost got her," he said. "Honey, wouldn't it be humiliating if we got you to like dick so much that you couldn't do without it? Just imagine, hunting for it in dark bars and dirty alleys, looking for a joystick to sit on, looking for some man with a big, hard dick to hold your legs apart and sink it in, being obsessed with cock, needing it and hating it at the same time. Coming around it. Being addicted to it. Needing it there to come around. Like you need it now, to come around, to fuck you and grind you down and make you holler and groan."

He put one foot up on the bed, then gradually insinuated the toe of his boot between her legs, nudging Mike's fingers aside. At the feel of that smooth boot leather against her clit, she couldn't hold back any more. She mashed her pussy down onto it, cried to be fucked, and came each time Mike's long cock slammed past her cervix. "At least," she thought, "I didn't come for this fucker behind me, I came because Don's boot was pressing against me." It was small consolation. The humiliation lingered, and it lit a fire that made her orgasm dwindle into irritation. She wanted more.

119

Joe came back with a paper cup of water and held it for her to drink while Mike turned her loose. When he went to remove the nipple clamps, Don said, "Don't. Leave them on. You, cunt. Go squat and piss."

She trotted into the bathroom and left the door open without being told. It was hard to get it started, with her insides rearranged and all of them staring at her. Finally, a hot stream spurted out. Before she got a chance to wipe herself, Don had her in handcuffs and headed toward the cage. He was impatient to get going. That meant he was planning to have a lot of fun. Shit. "You two just climb into bed and amuse yourselves," he called over his shoulder.

He opened the cage door and thrust her inside, locked it, then reached through the bars for her tits. He had some chain and padlocks in his hand. In seconds, she was chained to the bars by her tits. Her ass pressed against the bars on the opposite side of the cage. He removed one handcuff, passed it around a bar, and put it back around her wrist. She could not straighten up because of the way her tits were chained, and she could not crouch either. Her ass was held in an inviting position, and with her hands cuffed behind her back, there was nothing she could do about it. Except suffer. Which she did, grudgingly.

She could only see part of the bed. Joe's hands were twined in Mike's hair, and he was urging Mike to suck harder. Sweat ran down his thickly furred chest and made his abs glisten. Mike's hands were busy below his waist, and Joe growled, "If you come in your hand, I'm going to make you eat it off your fingers."

Her jailer examined her through the bars. He prodded her experimentally with the smooth, rounded end of a wooden truncheon. She moved a little, but the tug on her nipples made her wish immediately that she had not.

"You are my prisoner," he said softly. "Cop-meat. And I'm going to fuck you. Guess where." His gloved hand fondly squeezed her buttock. "This is something I've wanted for a long time. But I really do want you to enjoy it. That makes it better for me, and more embarrassing for you. So I'm going to get you ready." He showed her the well-greased butt plug. She averted her eyes. She always found the bright pink rubber they made sex toys out of garish, even offensive. It made them seem silly. Well, she wouldn't have to look at it, because he was pushing it into her. True to his word, it didn't hurt—just discomfited. Once she felt her anus close around the small neck of the plug, he moved her rear end over a little, so that a cold steel bar pressed into the cleft of her buttocks. "If you wiggle up against that," he said, "you should get yourself warmed up real nice." He regarded her in silence for a few seconds, then said, "What's the matter? I've got two more, size large and extra-large, if you need any more encouragement."

120

Pat Califia

It's odd, she reflected, how you can get into a scene and lose some of your inhibitions and go crazy, and while it's happening, you think you'll do anything, but of course you won't. There's always a hitch, always another barrier you don't want to cross, another step that somebody has to push you down. I hate his guts, and I will not squirm around on this horrid thing while he stands there staring at me and jerking off. Fuck him.

"You stubborn, stupid, ungrateful, ill-trained bitch," he cursed. "I don't know why I bother. But if you think you're going to start holding out on me at this stage of the game, shit-head, you better think again."

A puff of air cooled her backside, and she realized she was dripping with sweat and that both of her shining, wet ass cheeks protruded slightly outside the frame of the cell. Then the source of the cool breeze—the doubled-up belt—landed on her butt, and there was no thinking, only pain. Not only was she crying out with each solid, flat impact of the belt, she was moving her ass, provocatively, helplessly.

from "The Surprise Party"

He didn't have much of her to work on, so there was no hope that he would alternate blows upon her thighs and shoulders with the blows to her ass. Concentrated in such a small area, the beating hurt worse than it would have otherwise. There was no respite to gather courage and breath. So she tried to curve her lower back and thrust more of her ass through the bars, adding just another inch of available skin to spread the pain out and make it easier to take. She succeeded (at the cost of drawing her nipples out to maximum tautness in the clamps) in flattening her thighs against the bars, and the belt kissed them for a few seconds, but returned inexorably to her ass.

Oh, yes, he was good. Thorough, hard, unstoppable. She had the feeling he could go on and on until she was deeply bruised, then bleeding, then showing bare bone through her flayed and shredded flesh. The pain was lightning in the marrow of her bones. And the animal noises she was making, the sweat flying into her eyes, hurt her pride just as much as the flying belt hurt her ass.

Under severe and continuous pain, the soul reaches a certain kind of clarity. Confusion and hope cannot be tolerated. Anything that deflects energy from withstanding the pain becomes useless, impossible to hang onto. Such ballast is jettisoned automatically. Pride (which clenches muscles and makes blows bruise instead of merely sting, which stiffens the neck and thickens the tongue until one cannot plead for mercy, which forbids the use of any clever, demeaning slave ploy to cajole the master and stay his anger) is the first thing to be thrown overboard.

After all, what justification is there for pride when you are locked in a cage, your breasts are suffering, your hands are locked behind your back, your ass has been filled by a foreign object, and someone is beating you black and blue? Your bestial need to survive the ordeal in one piece makes pride superfluous. And the seeping fluid of sexual arousal that makes your thighs slip together as he punishes you makes pride seem hypocritical, not to mention pretentious.

No, it is better to scream freely, without restraint, to plead for mercy, to cry, to struggle beautifully, to sweat and strain, to be marked and marked again, to ask him what he wants, to agree to everything he says, to ask for more if that is what he wants, to confess, to grunt like a pig or howl like a dog, to promise anything—anything—if only it will stop.

Once the emotions have been simplified and the illusion of free will destroyed, the body also needs to purge itself. Dancing under agony, scant attention is left to control any sphincter or restrain excretion until it can be performed in a seemly, civilized manner.

Now he was using a very thin riding crop. The pain escalated sharply. From the feel of it, it had a whalebone core. It was horrifying. Beyond expressing with a mere scream. She was convinced that the sweat rolling down her legs must be blood, knowing that it most certainly was not. It was too much—too much—too much for decency—

So she pissed. Uncontrollably. From fear and anguish. All over herself, the floor of the cage, and anything else close enough to get splashed.

Then he was enraged, as yellow drops of her urine beaded up on the toes of his mirror-shiny boots, and the strokes he laid on then with that evil, skinny crop made her shimmy as though she were possessed and yell until she lost her voice.

When it stopped, she felt as if she were in the eye of a hurricane. There was respite from pain, but not from drama or tension. The only question was, when would it start again, and how? She hung her head, weeping, in fact blinded by tears, slobbering and sweating, her nose dripping snot, every pore and orifice opened up, wet, and slack. If it were not for her tit clamps and the steel circlets around her wrists, she would have slid to the floor and passed out.

His hands were lifting the swollen masses of her buttocks, moving them to one side of the bar that had divided them, his fingertips admiring this or that particularly purple spot. "Say that you love me," he said, intense and tender.

"I love you," she sobbed. What broken-hearted prisoner does not love her torturer after a beating stops?

"Say that you're sorry."

"I—I'm sorry." She was blubbering now. God, how disgusting.

His questing fingers removed the butt plug—or rather, received it as it fell out of her. They probed—tentatively—and the by-now familiar feel of his rubber-clad erection against her raw cleft replaced his fingers.

122

Pat Califia

"Say you want me."

"I want you, sir."

"To do what?"

Surrender. Quivering. Bowing to the inevitable.

"To fuck my ass, sir."

"That's good. That's very good. I'd really like to." The leather-gloved hand was moving up and down his cock. She had never met a man who loved handling himself so much. The back of his moving hand pressed against her, making obscene insinuations. "Persuade me, cunt. Talk me into it. If you make it sound sweet enough, maybe I will...put this inside of you. But hurry. If you don't make it fast, I might come in my fist, and all this good hot stuff would go to waste. Talk to me, darlin'."

Talk to him? And why was this harder (well, just as hard) as squirming on a butt-plug to heat herself up for his cock? It was another barrier—but this time she recognized the danger, refused to postpone her pleasure or invite more punishment, and pushed the words out of her mouth as fast as she could.

It was not a very elegant confession, but it was effective. A few vulgar sentences, interrupted by her last few sobs and soft cries of pain when he pressed his big hands into her bruised hindquarters, persuaded him to push his thumbs, side-by-side, into her ass. Lubrication followed. It was cold and thick. Jesus, it was creepy, having something in there. It gave her goosebumps and made her skin crawl, that awkward feeling of needing to shit, the fear of pain in that most tender of all places, anxiety about being dirty—and despite all that, the fierce hope that his strong cock would follow his fingers and pierce her deeply, take pleasure in her ass.

"You're nice and snug," he murmured, smooth leather hands reaching through the bars to stroke her, hands returning to her ass to lift and separate the cheeks, massage the sides of her asshole, position his cock and push a little. She held still, letting him work on her, while her hands gripped the bars and tried to pull them apart. There was a popping sensation as the head of his dick slipped past her sphincter, then the smooth length of the shaft dilating—filling—

And the bastard had one hand around her waist, fiddling with her clit! Damn him! It was distracting. She wanted to be able to concentrate on the penetration. She wanted to feel her ass hugging and milking him, delighting him until he came. The possibility of coming herself was annoying.

He kept it up anyway, holding her firmly against the bars, then began to withdraw from her ass. There was a sensation of relief—oh, thank heaven, it's coming out—then dismay as he pushed his cock back in—oh, no, my ass is still full, it can't close up and get comfy, I need to shit, he's going to hurt me—

123

It seemed to go on forever. Apparently he could fuck her as long as he wanted to without losing control and coming. Damn. She twisted, pushed back when he pushed in, tried to get her hands free to stroke him, tried to twist her head around so she could see him, kiss him—

Impossible. "I can't touch you!" she cried in exasperation. His strokes speeded up. "Damn you, I can't move! My tits hurt—my ass hurts—let me go!" He panted, on the brink of forgetting about her and fucking her only to please himself. She told him in a fierce, insistent voice just how much he was hurting her by fucking her this way, how dirty it made her feel, how much she wanted his cock to hurt her, to use her, to let the cramping, clinging lining of her ass masturbate his cock. He groaned and gave up, then practically flew into her, battering her ass. His hands no longer felt for her clit. Instead, they squeezed her buttocks hard, until she screamed with anger and pain, and he came. Oh, oh, the way he came—the thought of that happening, up inside her ass, where he was so unwelcome and so much needed—made her shake with her own convulsions, a series of contractions that actually pulled the clips off her tits and left her seeing exploding stars that faded into clouds of red mist.

Pat Califia

Tom of
Finland

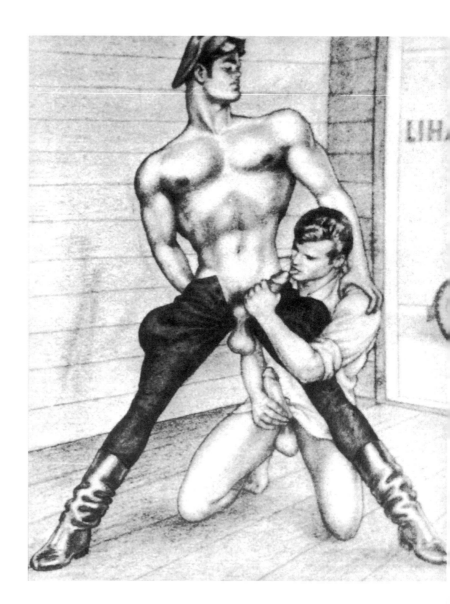

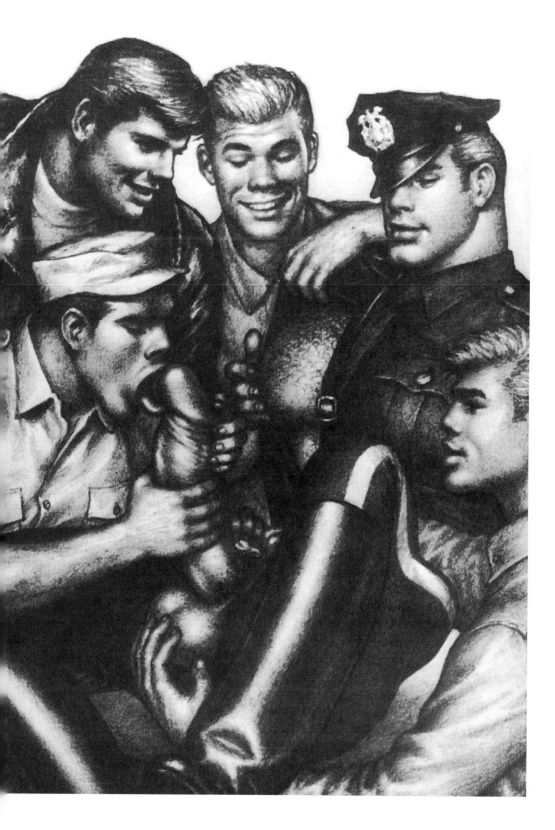

USE
A
RUBBER

129

from
Retrospective

© Tom-87

Eating the Other: Desire and Resistance from *Black Looks: Race and Representation*

BELL HOOKS

> This is theory's acute dilemma: that desire expresses itself most fully where only those absorbed in its delights and torments are present, that it triumphs most completely over other human preoccupations in places sheltered from view. Thus it is paradoxically in hiding that the secrets of desire come to light, that hegemonic impositions and their reversals, evasions, and subversions are at their most honest and active, and that the identities and disjunctures between felt passion and established culture place themselves on most vivid display.
>
> —Joan Cocks, *The Oppositional Imagination*

Within current debates about race and difference, mass culture is the contemporary location that both publicly declares and perpetuates the idea that there is pleasure to be found in the acknowledgment and enjoyment of racial difference. The commodification of Otherness has been so successful because it is offered as a new delight, more intense, more satisfying than normal ways of doing and feeling. Within commodity culture, ethnicity becomes spice, seasoning that can liven up the dull dish that is mainstream white culture. Cultural taboos around sexuality and desire are transgressed and made explicit as the media bombards folks with a message of difference no longer based on the white supremacist assumption that "blondes have more fun." The "real fun" is to be had by bringing to the surface all those "nasty" unconscious fantasies and longings about contact with the Other embedded in the secret (not so secret) deep structure of white supremacy. In many ways it is a contemporary revival of interest in the "primitive," with a distinctly postmodern slant. As Marianna Torgovnick argues in *Gone Primitive: Savage Intellects, Modern Lives*:

What is clear now is that the West's fascination with the primitive has to do with its own crises in identity, with its own need to clearly demarcate subject and object even while flirting with other ways of experiencing the universe.

Certainly from the standpoint of white supremacist capitalist patriarchy, the hope is that desires for the "primitive" or fantasies about the Other can be continually exploited, and that such exploitation will occur in a manner that reinscribes and maintains the *status quo*. Whether or not desire for contact with the Other, for connection rooted in the longing for pleasure, can act as a critical intervention challenging and subverting racist domination, inviting and enabling critical resistance, is an unrealized political possibility. Exploring how desire for the Other is expressed, manipulated, and transformed by encounters with difference and the different is a critical terrain that can indicate whether these potentially revolutionary longings are ever fulfilled.

Contemporary working-class British slang playfully converges the discourse of desire, sexuality, and the Other, evoking the phrase getting "a bit of the Other" as a way to speak about sexual encounter. Fucking is the Other. Displacing the notion of Otherness from race, ethnicity, skin-color, the body emerges as a site of contestation where sexuality is the metaphoric Other that threatens to take over, consume, transform *via* the experience of pleasure. Desired and sought after, sexual pleasure alters the consenting subject, deconstructing notions of will, control, coercive domination. Commodity culture in the United States exploits conventional thinking about race, gender, and sexual desire by "working" both the idea that racial difference marks one as Other and the assumption that sexual agency expressed within the context of racialized sexual encounter is a conversion experience that alters one's place and participation in contemporary cultural politics. The seductive promise of this encounter is that it will counter the terrorizing force of the *status quo* that makes identity fixed, static, a condition of containment and death. And that it is this willingness to transgress racial boundaries within the realm of the sexual that eradicates the fear that one must always conform to the norm to remain "safe." Difference can seduce precisely because the mainstream imposition of sameness is a provocation that terrorizes. And as Jean Baudrillard suggests in *Fatal Strategies*:

> Provocation—unlike seduction, which allows things to come into play and appear in secret, dual and ambiguous—does not leave you free to be; it calls on you to reveal yourself as you are. It is always blackmail by identity (and thus a symbolic murder, since you are never that, except precisely by being condemned to it).

bell hooks

To make one's self vulnerable to the seduction of difference, to seek an encounter with the Other, does not require that one relinquish forever one's mainstream positionality. When race and ethnicity become commodified as resources for pleasure, the culture of specific groups, as well as the bodies of individuals, can be seen as constituting an alternative playground where members of dominating races, genders, sexual practices affirm their power-over in intimate relations with the Other. While teaching at Yale, I walked one bright spring day in the downtown area of New Haven, which is close to campus and invariably brings one into contact with many of the poor black people who live nearby, and found myself walking behind a group of very blond, very white, jock type boys. (The downtown area was often talked about as an arena where racist domination of blacks by whites was contested on the sidewalks, as white people, usually male, often jocks, used their bodies to force black people off the sidewalk, to push our bodies aside, without ever looking at us or acknowledging our presence.) Seemingly unaware of my presence, these young men talked about their plans to fuck as many girls from other racial/ethnic groups as they could "catch" before graduation. They "ran" it down. Black girls were high on the list, Native American girls hard to find, Asian girls (all lumped into the same category), deemed easier to entice, were considered "prime targets." Talking about this overheard conversation with my students, I found that it was commonly accepted that one "shopped" for sexual partners in the same way one "shopped" for courses at Yale, and that race and ethnicity was a serious category on which selections were based.

To these young males and their buddies, fucking was a way to confront the Other, as well as a way to make themselves over, to leave behind white "innocence" and enter the world of "experience." As is often the case in this society, they were confident that non-white people had more life experience, were more worldly, sensual, and sexual because they were different. Getting a bit of the Other, in this case engaging in sexual encounters with non-white females, was considered a ritual of transcendence, a movement out into a world of difference that would transform, an acceptable rite of passage. The direct objective was not simply to sexually possess the Other; it was to be changed in some way by the encounter. "Naturally," the presence of the Other, the body of the Other, was seen as existing to serve the ends of white male desires. Writing about the way difference is recouped in the West in "The 'Primitive' Unconscious of Modern Art, or White Skin, Black Masks," Hal Foster reminds readers that Picasso regarded the tribal objects he had acquired as "witnesses" rather than as "models." Foster critiques this positioning of the Other, emphasizing that this recognition was "contingent upon instrumentality": "In this way, through affinity and use, the primitive is sent up into the service of the Western tradition (which is then seen to have partly produced it)." A similar critique can be made of contemporary trends in inter-racial sexual desire and contact initiated by white males. They claim the body of the colored Other instrumentally, as unexplored terrain, a symbolic frontier that will be fertile ground for their reconstruction of the masculine norm, for asserting themselves as transgressive desiring subjects. They call upon the Other to be both witness and participant in this transformation.

For white boys to openly discuss their desire for colored girls (or boys) publicly announces their break with a white supremacist past that would have such desire articulated only as taboo, as secret, as shame. They see their willingness to openly name their desire for the Other as affirmation of cultural plurality (its impact on sexual preference and choice). Unlike racist white men who historically violated the bodies of black women/women of color to assert their position as colonizer/conqueror, these young men see themselves as non-racists, who choose to transgress racial boundaries within the sexual realm not to dominate the Other, but rather so that they can be acted upon, so that they can be changed utterly. Not at all attuned to those aspects of their sexual fantasies that irrevocably link them to collective white racist domination, they believe their desire for contact represents a progressive change in white attitudes towards non-whites. They do not see themselves as perpetuating racism. To them the most potent indication of that change is the frank expression of longing, the open declaration of desire, the need to be intimate with dark Others. The point is to be changed by this convergence of pleasure and Otherness. One dares—acts—on the assumption that the exploration into the world of difference, into the body of the Other, will provide a greater, more intense pleasure than any that exists in the ordinary world of one's familiar racial group. And even though the conviction is that the familiar world will remain intact even as one ventures outside it, the hope is that they will reenter that world no longer the same.

The current wave of "imperialist nostalgia" (defined by Renato Rosaldo in *Culture and Truth* as "nostalgia, often found under imperialism, where people mourn the passing of what they themselves have transformed" or as "a process of yearning for what one has destroyed that is a form of mystification") often obscures contemporary cultural strategies deployed not to mourn but to celebrate the sense of a continuum of "primitivism." In mass culture, imperialist nostalgia takes the form of reenacting and reritualizing in different ways the imperialist, colonizing journey as narrative fantasy of power and desire, of seduction by the Other. This longing is rooted in the atavistic belief that the spirit of the "primitive" resides in the bodies of dark Others whose cultures, traditions and lifestyles may indeed be irrevocably changed by imperialism, colonization, and racist

133

domination. The desire to make contact with those bodies deemed Other, with no apparent will to dominate, assuages the guilt of the past, even takes the form of a defiant gesture where one denies accountability and historical connection. Most importantly, it establishes a contemporary narrative where the suffering imposed by structures of domination on those designated Other is deflected by an emphasis on seduction and longing where the desire is not to make the Other over in one's image but to become the Other.

Whereas mournful imperialist nostalgia constitutes the betrayed and abandoned world of the Other as an accumulation of lack and loss, contemporary longing for the "primitive" is expressed by the projection onto the Other of a sense of plenty, bounty, a field of dreams. Commenting on this strategy in "Readings in Cultural Resistance," Hal Foster contends, "Difference is thus used productively; indeed, in a social order which seems to know no outside (and which must contrive its own transgressions to redefine its limits), difference is often fabricated in the interests of social control as well as of commodity innovation." Masses of young people dissatisfied by U.S. imperialism, unemployment, lack of economic opportunity, afflicted by the postmodern malaise of alienation, no sense of grounding, no redemptive identity, can be manipulated by cultural strategies that offer Otherness as appeasement, particularly through commodification. The contemporary crises of identity in the West, especially as experienced by white youth, are eased when the "primitive" is recouped via a focus on diversity and pluralism which suggests the Other can provide life-sustaining alternatives. Concurrently, diverse ethnic/racial groups can also embrace this sense of specialness, that histories and experience once seen as worthy only of disdain can be looked upon with awe.

Cultural appropriation of the Other assuages feelings of deprivation and lack that assault the psyches of radical white youth who choose to be disloyal to Western civilization. Concurrently, marginalized groups, deemed Other, who have been ignored, rendered invisible, can be seduced by the emphasis on Otherness, by its commodification, because it offers the promise of recognition and reconciliation. When the dominant culture demands that the Other be offered as sign that progressive political change is taking place, that the American Dream can indeed be inclusive of difference, it invites a resurgence of essentialist cultural nationalism. The acknowledged Other must assume recognizable forms. Hence, it is not African American culture formed in resistance to contemporary situations that surfaces, but nostalgic evocation of a "glorious" past. And even though the focus is often on the ways that this past was "superior" to the present, this cultural narrative relies on stereotypes of the "primitive," even as it eschews the term, to evoke a world where black people were in harmony with nature and with one another. This narrative is linked to white

bell hooks

Western conceptions of the dark Other, not to a radical questioning of those representations.

Should youth of any other color not know how to move closer to the Other, or how to get in touch with the "primitive," consumer culture promises to show the way. It is within the commercial realm of advertising that the drama of Otherness finds expression. Encounters with Otherness are clearly marked as more exciting, more intense, and more threatening. The lure is the combination of pleasure and danger. In the cultural marketplace the Other is coded as having the capacity to be more alive, as holding the secret that will allow those who venture and dare to break with the cultural anhedonia (defined in Sam Keen's *The Passionate Life* as "the insensitivity to pleasure, the incapacity for experiencing happiness") and experience sensual and spiritual renewal. Before his untimely death, Michel Foucault, the quintessential transgressive thinker in the West, confessed that he had real difficulties experiencing pleasure:

> I think that pleasure is a very difficult behavior. It's not as simple as that to enjoy one's self. And I must say that's my dream. I would like and I hope I die of an overdose of pleasure of any kind. Because I think it's really difficult and I always have the feeling that I do not feel *the* pleasure, the complete total pleasure and, for me, it's related to death. Because I think that the kind of pleasure I would consider as the real pleasure, would be so deep, so intense, so overwhelming that I couldn't survive it. I would die.

Though speaking from the standpoint of his individual experience, Foucault voices a dilemma felt by many in the West. It is precisely that longing for *the* pleasure that has led the white West to sustain romantic fantasy of the "primitive" and the concrete search for a real primitive paradise, whether that location be a country or a body, dark continent or dark flesh, perceived as the perfect embodiment of that possibility.

Within this fantasy of Otherness, the longing for pleasure projected as a force that can disrupt and subvert the will to dominate it acts to both mediate and challenge. In Lorraine Hansberry's play *Les Blancs*, it is the desire to experience closeness and community that leads the white American journalist Charles to make contact and tempt to establish a friendship with Tshembe, the black revolutionary. Charles struggles to divest himself of white supremacist privilege, eschews the role of colonizer, and refuses racist exoticization of blacks. Yet he continues to assume that he alone can decide the nature of his relationship to a black person. Evoking the idea of a universal transcendent subject, he appeals to Tshembe by repudiating the role of oppressor, declaring, "I am a man who feels like talking." When

Tshembe refuses to accept the familiar relationship offered him, refuses to satisfy Charles' longing for camaraderie and contact, he is accused of hating white men. Calling attention to situations where white people have oppressed other white people, Tshembe challenges Charles, declaring that "race is a device—no more, no less," that "it explains nothing all." Pleased with this disavowal of the importance of race, Charles agrees, stating "race hasn't a thing to do with it." Tshembe then deconstructs the category "race" without minimizing or ignoring the impact of racism, telling him:

> I believe in the recognition of devices as *devices*—but I also believe in the reality of those devices. In one century men choose to hide their conquests under religion, in another under race. So you and I may recognize the fraudulence of the device in both cases, but the fact remains that a man who has a sword run through him because he will not become a Moslem or a Christian—or who is lynched in Mississippi or Zatembe because he is black—is suffering the utter reality of that device of conquest. And it is pointless to pretend that it doesn't exist merely because it is a lie...

Again and again Tshembe must make it clear to Charles that subject to subject contact between white and black which signals the absence of domination, of an oppressor/oppressed relationship, must emerge through mutual choice and negotiation. That simply by expressing their desire for "intimate" contact with black people, white people do not eradicate the politics of racial domination as they are made manifest in personal interaction.

Mutual recognition of racism, its impact both on those who are dominated and those who dominate, is the only standpoint that makes possible an encounter between races that is not based on denial and fantasy. For it is the ever present reality of racist domination, of white supremacy, that renders problematic the desire of white people to have contact with the Other. Often it is this reality that is most masked when representations of contact between white and non-white, white and black, appear in mass culture. One area where the politics of diversity and its concomitant insistence on inclusive representation have had serious impact is advertising. Now that sophisticated market surveys reveal the extent to which poor and materially underprivileged people of all races/ethnicities consume products, sometimes in a quantity disproportionate to income, it has become more evident that these markets can be appealed to with advertising. Market surveys revealed that black people buy more Pepsi than other soft drinks and suddenly we see more Pepsi commercials with black people in them.

The world of fashion has also come to understand that selling products is heightened by the exploitation of Otherness. The success of Benneton

136

bell hooks

ads, which with their racially diverse images have become a model for various advertising strategies epitomize this trend. Many ads that focus on Otherness make no explicit comments, or rely solely on visual messages, but the recent fall Tweeds catalogue provides an excellent example of the way contemporary culture exploits notions of Otherness with both visual images and text. The catalogue cover shows a map of Egypt. Inserted into the heart of the country, so to speak, is a photo of a white male (an *Out of Africa* type) holding an Egyptian child in his arms. Behind them is not the scenery of Egypt as modern city, but rather shadowy silhouettes resembling huts and palm trees. Inside, the copy quotes Gustave Flaubert's comments from *Flaubert in Egypt.* For seventy-five pages Egypt becomes a landscape of dreams, and its darker-skinned people background, scenery to highlight whiteness, and the longing of whites to inhabit, if only for a time, the world of the Other. The front page copy declares:

> We did not want our journey to be filled with snapshots of an antique land. Instead, we wanted to rediscover our clothing in the context of a different culture. Was it possible, we wondered, to express our style in an unaccustomed way, surrounded by Egyptian colors, Egyptian textures, even bathed in an ancient Egyptian light?

Is this not imperialist nostalgia at its best—potent expression of longing for the "primitive"? One desires "a bit of the Other" to enhance the blank landscape of whiteness. Nothing is said in the text about Egyptian people, yet their images are spread throughout its pages. Often their faces are blurred by the camera, a strategy which ensures that readers will not become more enthralled by the images of Otherness than those of whiteness. The point of this photographic attempt at defamiliariation is to distance us from whiteness, so that we will return to it more intently.

In most of the "snapshots," all carefully selected and posed, there is no mutual looking. One desires contact with the Other even as one wishes boundaries to remain intact. When bodies contact one another, touch, it is almost always a white hand doing the touching, white hands that rest on the bodies of colored people, unless the Other is a child. One snapshot of "intimate" contact shows two women with their arms linked, the way close friends might link arms. One is an Egyptian woman identified by a caption that reads "with her husband and baby, Ahmedio A'bass, twenty-two, leads a gypsy's life"; the second woman is a white-skinned model. The linked hands suggest that these two women share something, have a basis of contact and indeed they do, they resemble one another, look more alike than different. The message again is that "primitivism," though more apparent in the Other, also resides in the white self. It is not the world of Egypt, of

137

Eating the Other: Desire and Resistance

"gypsy" life, that is affirmed by this snapshot, but the ability of white people to roam the world, making contact. Wearing pants while standing next to her dark "sister" who wears a traditional skirt, the white woman appears to be cross-dressing (an ongoing theme in Tweeds). Visually the image suggests that she and first world white women like her are liberated, have greater freedom to roam than darker women who live peripatetic lifestyles.

Significantly, the catalogue that followed this one focused on Norway. There the people of Norway are not represented, only the scenery. Are we to assume that white folks from this country are as at "home" in Norway as they are here so there is no need for captions and explanations? In this visual text, whiteness is the unifying feature—not culture. Of course, for Tweeds to exploit Otherness to dramatize "whiteness" while in Egypt, it cannot include darker-skinned models since the play on contrasts that is meant to highlight "whiteness" could not happen nor could the exploitation that urges consumption of the Other whet the appetite in quite the same way; just as inclusion of darker-skinned models in the Norway issue might suggest that the West is not as unified by whiteness as this visual text suggests. Essentially speaking, both catalogues evoke a sense that white people are homogeneous and share "white bread culture."

Those progressive white intellectuals who are particularly critical of "essentialist" notions of identity when writing about mass culture, race, and gender have not focused their critiques on white identity and the way essentialism informs representations of whiteness. It is always the non-white, or in some cases the non-heterosexual Other, who is guilty of essentialism. Few white intellectuals call attention to the way in which the contemporary obsession with white consumption of the dark Other has served as a catalyst for the resurgence of essentialist based racial and ethnic nationalism. Black nationalism, with its emphasis on black separatism, is resurging as a response to the assumption that white cultural imperialism and white yearning to possess the Other are invading black life, appropriating and violating black culture. As a survival strategy, black nationalism surfaces most strongly when white cultural appropriation of black culture threatens to decontextualize and thereby erase knowledge of the specific historical and social context of black experience from which cultural productions and distinct black styles emerge. Yet most white intellectuals writing critically about black culture do not see these constructive dimensions of black nationalism and tend to see it instead as naïve essentialism, rooted in notions of ethnic purity that resemble white racist assumptions.

In the essay "Hip, and the Long Front of Color," white critic Andrew Ross interprets Langston Hughes' declaration ("You've taken my blues and gone—You sing 'em on Broadway—And you sing 'em in Hollywood Bowl—And you mixed 'em up with symphonies—And you fixed 'em—So they

138

bell hooks

don't sound like me. Yep, you done taken my blues and gone.") as a "complaint" that "celebrates...folk purism." Yet Hughes' declaration can be heard as a critical comment on appropriation (not a complaint). A distinction must be made between the longing for ongoing cultural recognition of the creative source of particular African American cultural productions that emerge from distinct black experience, and essentialist investments in notions of ethnic purity that undergird crude versions of black nationalism.

Currently, the commodification of difference promotes paradigms of consumption wherein whatever difference the Other inhabits is eradicated, *via* exchange, by a consumer cannibalism that not only displaces the Other but denies the significance of that Other's history through a process of decontextualization. Like the "primitivism" Hal Foster maintains "absorbs the primitive, in part *via* the concept of affinity," contemporary notions of "crossover" expand the parameters of cultural production to enable the voice of the non-white Other to be heard by a larger audience even as it denies the specificity of that voice, or as it recoups it for its own use.

This scenario is played out in the film *Heart Condition* when Mooney, a white racist cop, has a heart transplant and receives a heart from Stone, a black man he has been trying to destroy because Stone has seduced Chris, the white call girl that Mooney loves. Transformed by his new "black heart," Mooney learns how to be more seductive, changes his attitudes towards race, and, in perfect Hollywood style, wins the girl in the end. Unabashedly dramatizing a process of "eating the Other" (in ancient religious practices among so called "primitive" people, the heart of a person may be ripped out and eaten so that one can embody that person's spirit or special characteristics), a film like *Heart Condition* addresses the fantasies of a white audience. At the end of the film, Mooney, reunited with Chris through marriage and surrounded by Stone's caring black kin, has become the "father" of Chris and Stone's bi-racial baby who is dark-skinned, the color of his father. Stone, whose ghost has haunted Mooney, is suddenly "history"—gone. Interestingly, this mainstream film suggests that patriarchal struggle over "ownership" (i.e., sexual possession of white women's bodies) is the linchpin of racism. Once Mooney can accept and bond with Stone on the phallocentric basis of their mutual possession and "desire" for Chris, their homosocial bonding makes brotherhood possible and eradicates the racism that has kept them apart. Significantly, patriarchal bonding mediates and becomes the basis for the eradication of racism.

In part, this film offers a version of racial pluralism that challenges racism by suggesting that the white male's life will be richer, more pleasurable, if he accepts diversity. Yet it also offers a model of change that still leaves a white supremacist capitalist patriarchy intact, though no longer based on coercive domination of black people. It insists that white male desire must be sustained by the "labor" (in this case the heart) of a dark Other. The fantasy, of course, is that this labor will no longer be exacted *via* domination, but will be given willingly. Not surprisingly, most black folks talked about this film as "racist." The young desirable handsome intelligent black male (who we are told *via* his own self-portrait is "hung like a shetland pony") must die so that the aging white male can both restore his potency (he awakens from the transplant to find a replica of a huge black penis standing between his legs) and be more sensitive and loving. Torgovnick reminds readers in *Gone Primitive* that a central element in the Western fascination with primitivism is its focus on "overcoming alienation from the body, restoring the body, and hence the self, to a relation of full and easy harmony with nature or the cosmos." It is this conceptualization of the "primitive" and the black male as quintessential representative that is dramatized in *Heart Condition*. One weakness in Torgovnick's work is her refusal to recognize how deeply the idea of the "primitive" is entrenched in the psyches of everyday people, shaping contemporary racist stereotypes, perpetuating racism. When she suggests, "our own culture by and large rejects the association of blackness with rampant sexuality and irrationality, with decadence and corruption, with disease and death," one can only wonder what culture she is claiming as her own.

Films like *Heart Condition* make black culture and black life backdrop, scenery for narratives that essentially focus on white people. Nationalist black voices critique this cultural crossover, its decentering of black experience as it relates to black people, and its insistence that it is acceptable for whites to explore blackness as long as their ultimate agenda is appropriation. Politically "on the case" when they critique white cultural appropriation of black experience that reinscribes it within a "cool" narrative of white supremacy, these voices can not be dismissed as naïve. They are misguided when they suggest that white cultural imperialism is best critiqued and resisted by black separatism, or when they evoke outmoded notions of ethnic purity that deny the way in which black people exist in the West, are Western, and are at times positively influenced by aspects of white culture.

Steve Perry's essay "The Politics of Crossover" deconstructs notions of racial purity by outlining the diverse inter-cultural exchanges between black and white musicians, yet he seems unable to acknowledge that this reality does not alter the fact that white cultural imperialist appropriation of black culture maintains white supremacy and is a constant threat to black liberation. Even though Perry can admit that successful black crossover artists, such as Prince, carry the "crossover impulse" to the point where it "begins to be a denial of blackness," he is unable to see this as threatening to black people who are daily resisting racism, advocating ongoing decolonization, and in need of an effective black liberation struggle.

bell hooks

Underlying Perry's condescension, and at times contemptuous attitude towards all expressions of black nationalism, is a traditional leftist insistence on the primacy of class over race. This standpoint inhibits his capacity to understand the specific political needs of black people that are addressed, however inadequately, by essentialist-based black separatism. As Howard Winant clarifies in "Postmodern Racial Politics in the United States: Difference and Inequality," one must understand race to understand class because "in the postmodern political framework of the contemporary United States, hegemony is determined by the articulation of race and class." And most importantly it is the "ability of the right to represent class issues in racial terms" that is "central to the current pattern of conservative hegemony." Certainly an essentialist-based black nationalism imbued with and perpetuating many racial stereotypes is an inadequate and ineffective response to the urgent demand that there be renewed and viable revolutionary black liberation struggle that would take radical politicization of black people, strategies of decolonization, critiques of capitalism, and ongoing resistance to racist domination as its central goals.

Resurgence of black nationalism as an expression of black people's desire to guard against white cultural appropriation indicates the extent to which the commodification of blackness (including the nationalist agenda) has been reinscribed and marketed with an atavistic narrative, a fantasy of Otherness that reduces protest to spectacle and stimulates even greater longing for the "primitive." Given this cultural context, black nationalism is more a gesture of powerlessness than a sign of critical resistance. Who can take seriously Public Enemy's insistence that the dominated and their allies "fight the power" when that declaration is in no way linked to a collective organized struggle. When young black people mouth 1960s' black nationalist rhetoric, don Kente cloth, gold medallions, dread their hair, and diss the white folks they hang out with, they expose the way meaningless commodification strips these signs of political integrity and meaning, denying the possibility that they can serve as a catalyst for concrete political action. As signs, their power to ignite critical consciousness is diffused when they are commodified. Communities of resistance are replaced by communities of consumption. As Stuart and Elizabeth Ewen emphasize in *Channels of Desire:*

> The politics of consumption must be understood as something more than what to buy, or even what to boycott. Consumption is a social relationship, the dominant relationship in our society—one that makes it harder and harder for people to hold together, to create community. At a time when for many of us the possibility of meaningful change seems to elude our grasp, it is a question of

141

Eating the Other: Desire and Resistance

immense social and political proportions. To establish popular initiative, consumerism must be transcended—a difficult but central task facing all people who still seek a better way of life.

Work by black artists that is overtly political and radical is rarely linked to an oppositional political culture. When commodified it is easy for consumers to ignore political messages. And even though a product like rap articulates narratives of coming to critical political consciousness, it also exploits stereotypes and essentialist notions of blackness (like black people have natural rhythm and are more sexual). The television show *In Living Color* is introduced by lyrics that tell listeners "do what you wanna do." Positively, this show advocates transgression, yet it negatively promotes racist stereotypes, sexism, and homophobia. Black youth culture comes to stand for the outer limits of "outness." The commercial nexus exploits the culture's desire (expressed by whites and blacks) to inscribe blackness as "primitive" sign, as wildness, and with it the suggestion that black people have secret access to intense pleasure, particularly pleasures of the body. It is the young black male body that is seen as epitomizing this promise of wildness, of unlimited physical prowess and unbridled eroticism. It was this black body that was most "desired" for its labor in slavery, and it is this body that is most represented in contemporary popular culture as the body to be watched, imitated, desired, possessed. Rather than a sign of pleasure in daily life outside the realm of consumption, the young black male body is represented most graphically as the body in pain.

Regarded fetishisticly in the psycho-sexual racial imagination of youth culture, the real bodies of young black men are daily viciously assaulted by white racist violence, black on black violence, the violence of overwork, and the violence of addiction and disease. In her introduction to *The Body in Pain*, Elaine Scarry states that "there is ordinarily no language for pain," that "physical pain is difficult to express; and that this inexpressibility has political consequences." This is certainly true of black male pain. Black males are unable to fully articulate and acknowledge the pain in their lives. They do not have a public discourse or audience within racist society that enables them to give their pain a hearing. Sadly, black men often evoke racist rhetoric that identifies the black male as animal, speaking of themselves as "endangered species," as "primitive," in their bid to gain recognition of their suffering.

When young black men acquire a powerful public voice and presence *via* cultural production, as has happened with the explosion of rap music, it does not mean that they have a vehicle that will enable them to articulate that pain. Providing narratives that are mainly about power and pleasure, that advocate resistance to racism yet support phallocentrism, rap denies

bell hooks

this pain. True, it was conditions of suffering and survival, of poverty, deprivation, and lack that characterized the marginal locations from which breakdancing and rap emerged. Described as "rituals" by participants in the poor urban non-white communities where they first took place, these practices offered individuals a means to gain public recognition and voice. Much of the psychic pain that black people experience daily in a white supremacist context is caused by dehumanizing oppressive forces, forces that render us invisible and deny us recognition. Michael H. (commenting on style in Stuart Ewen's book *All Consuming Images*) also talks about this desire for attention, stating that breakdancing and rap are a way to say "listen to my story, about myself, life, and romance." Rap music provides a public voice for young black men who are usually silenced and overlooked. It emerged in the streets—outside the confines of a domesticity shaped and informed by poverty, outside enclosed spaces where young males' bodies had to be contained and controlled.

In its earliest stages, rap was "a male thing." Young black and brown males could not breakdance and rap in cramped living spaces. Male creativity, expressed in rap and dancing, required wide-open spaces, symbolic frontiers where the body could do its thing, expand, grow, and move, surrounded by a watching crowd. Domestic space, equated with repression and containment, as well as with the "feminine" was resisted and rejected so that an assertive patriarchal paradigm of competitive masculinity and its concomitant emphasis on physical prowess could emerge. As a result, much rap music is riddled with sexism and misogyny. The public story of black male lives narrated by rap music speaks directly to and against white racist domination, but only indirectly hints at the enormity of black male pain. Constructing the black male body as site of pleasure and power, rap and the dances associated with it suggest vibrancy, intensity, and an unsurpassed joy in living. It may very well be that living on the edge, so close to the possibility of being "exterminated" (which is how many young black males feel) heightens one's ability to risk and makes one's pleasure more intense. It is this charge, generated by the tension between pleasure and danger, death and desire, that Foucault evokes when he speaks of that *complete total pleasure* that is related to death. Though Foucault is speaking as an individual, his words resonate in a culture affected by anhedonia—the inability to feel pleasure. In the United States, where our senses are daily assaulted and bombarded to such an extent that an emotional numbness sets in, it may take being "on the edge" for individuals to feel intensely. Hence the overall tendency in the culture is to see young black men as both dangerous and desirable.

Certainly the relationship between the experience of Otherness, of pleasure and death, is explored in the film *The Cook, the Thief, His Wife and Her*

Lover, which critiques white male imperialist domination even though this dimension of the movie was rarely mentioned when it was discussed in this country. Reviewers of the film did not talk about the representation of black characters, one would have assumed from such writing that the cast was all white and British. Yet black males are a part of the community of subordinates who are dominated by one controlling white man. After he has killed her lover, his blond white wife speaks to the dark-skinned cook, who clearly represents non-white immigrants, about the links between death and pleasure. It is he who explains to her the way blackness is viewed in the white imagination. The cook tells her that black foods are desired because they remind those who eat them of death, and that this is why they cost so much. When they are eaten (in the film, always and only by white people), the cook as native informant tells us it is a way to flirt with death, to flaunt one's power. He says that to eat black food is a way to say "death, I am eating you" and thereby conquering fear and acknowledging power. White racism, imperialism, and sexist domination prevail by courageous consumption. It is by eating the Other (in this case, death) that one asserts power and privilege.

A similar confrontation may be taking place within popular culture in this society as young white people seek contact with dark Others. They may long to conquer their fear of darkness and death. On the reactionary right, white youth may be simply seeking to affirm "white power" when they flirt with having contact with the Other. Yet there are many white youths who desire to move beyond whiteness. Critical of white imperialism and "into" difference, they desire cultural spaces where boundaries can be transgressed, where new and alternative relations can be formed. These desires are dramatized by two contemporary films, John Waters' *Hairspray* and the more recent film by Jim Jarmusch, *Mystery Train.* In *Hairspray,* the "cool" white people, working-class Traci and her middle-class boyfriend, transgress class and race boundaries to dance with black folks. She says to him as they stand in a rat-infested alley with winos walking about, "I wish I was dark-skinned." And he replies, "Traci, our souls are black even though our skin is white." Blackness—the culture, the music, the people—is once again associated with pleasure as well as death and decay. Yet their recognition of the particular pleasures and sorrows black folks experience does not lead to cultural appropriation but to an appreciation that extends into the realm of the political—Traci dares to support racial integration. In this film, the longing and desire whites express for contact with black culture is coupled with the recognition of the culture's value. One does not transgress boundaries to stay the same, to reassert white domination. *Hairspray* is nearly unique in its attempt to construct a fictive universe where white working class "undesirables" are in solidarity with black people. When Traci ays she wants to be black, blackness becomes a metaphor for freedom, an end to boundaries. Blackness is vital not because it represents the "primitive" but because it invites engagement in a revolutionary ethos that dares to challenge and disrupt the *status quo*. Like white rappers MC Search and Prime Minister Pete Nice who state that they "want to bring forth some sort of positive message to black people, that there are white people out here who understand what this is all about, who understand we have to get past all the hatred," Traci shifts her positionality to stand in solidarity with black people. She is concerned about her freedom and sees her liberation linked to black liberation and an effort to end racist domination.

Expressing a similar solidarity with the agenda of "liberation," which includes freedom to transgress, Sandra Bernhard, in her new film *Without You I'm Nothing*, also associates blackness with this struggle. In the March issue of *Interview* she says that the movie has "this whole black theme, which is like a personal metaphor for being on the outside." This statement shows that Bernhard's sense of blackness is both problematic and complex. The film opens with her pretending she is black. Dressed in African clothing, she renders problematic the question of race and identity, for this representation suggests that racial identity can be socially constructed even as it implies that cultural appropriation falls short because it is always imitation, fake. Conversely, she contrasts her attempt to be a black woman in drag with the black female's attempt to imitate a white female look. Bernhard's film suggests that alternative white culture derives its standpoint, its impetus from black culture. Identifying herself with marginalized Others, Bernhard's Jewish heritage as well as her sexually ambiguous erotic practices are experiences that already place her outside the mainstream. Yet the film does not clarify the nature of her identification with black culture. Throughout the film, she places herself in a relationship of comparison and competition with black women, seemingly exposing white female envy of black women and their desire to "be" imitation black women; yet she also pokes fun at black females. The unidentified black woman who appears in the film, like a phantom, looking at herself in the mirror has no name and no voice. Yet her image is always contrasted with that of Bernhard. Is she the fantasy Other Bernhard desires to become? Is she the fantasy Other Bernhard desires? The last scene of the film seems to confirm that black womanhood is the yardstick Bernhard uses to measure herself. Though she playfully suggests in the film that the work of black women singers like Nina Simone and Diana Ross is derivative, "stolen" from her work, this inversion of reality ironically calls attention to the way white women have "borrowed" from black women without acknowledging the debt they owe. In many ways, the film critiques white cultural appropriation of "blackness" that leaves no trace. Indeed, Bernhard identifies that she had her

Eating the
Other:
Desire and
Resistance

artistic beginnings working in black clubs, among black people. Though acknowledging where she is coming from, the film shows Bernhard clearly defining an artistic performance space that only she as a white woman can inhabit. Black women have no public, paying audience for our funny imitations of white girls. Indeed, it is difficult to imagine any setting other than an all black space where black women could use comedy to critique and ridicule white womanhood in the way Bernhard mocks black womanhood.

Closing the scene shrouded in a cloak that resembles an American flag, Bernhard unveils her nearly nude body. The film ends with the figure of the black woman, who has heretofore only been in the background, foregrounded as the only remaining audience watching this seductive performance. As though she is seeking acknowledgment of her identity, her power, Bernhard stares at the black woman, who returns her look with a contemptuous gaze. As if this look of disinterest and dismissal is not enough to convey her indifference, she removes a tube of red lipstick from her purse and writes on the table "fuck Sandra Bernhard." Her message seems to be: "You may need black culture since without us you are nothing, but black women have no need of you." In the film, all the white women strip, flaunt their sexuality, and appear to be directing their attention to a black male gaze. It is this standpoint that the film suggests may lead them to ignore black women and only notice what black women think of them when we are "right up in their face."

bell hooks

Bernhard's film walks a critical tightrope. On one hand it mocks white appropriation of black culture, white desire for black (as in the scene where Bernhard with a blond white girl persona is seen being "boned" by a black man whom we later find is mainly concerned about his hair—i.e., his own image) even as the film works as spectacle largely because of the clever ways Bernhard "uses" black culture and standard racial stereotypes. Since so many of the representations of blackness in the film are stereotypes it does not really go against the Hollywood cinematic grain. And like the Tweeds catalogue on Egypt, ultimately black people are reduced, as Bernhard declares in *Interview,* to "a personal metaphor." Blackness is the backdrop of Otherness she uses to insist on and clarify her status as Other, as cool, hip, and transgressive. Even though she lets audiences know that as an entertainment "rookie" she had her start working in close association with black people, the point is to name where she begins to highlight how far she has come. When Bernhard "arrives," able to exploit Otherness in a big time way, she arrives alone, not in the company of black associates. They are scenery, backdrop, background. Yet the end of the film problematizes this leave-taking. Is Bernhard leaving black folks or has she been rejected and dismissed? Maybe it's mutual. Like her entertainment cohort Madonna, Bernhard leaves her encounters with the Other richer than she was at the onset. We have no idea how the Other leaves her.

When I began thinking and doing research for this piece, I talked to folks from various locations about whether they thought the focus on race, Otherness, and difference in mass culture was challenging racism. There was overall agreement that the message that acknowledgment and exploration of racial difference can be pleasurable represents a breakthrough, a challenge to white supremacy, to various systems of domination. The overriding fear is that cultural, ethnic, and racial differences will be continually commodified and offered up as new dishes to enhance the white palate— that the Other will be eaten, consumed, and forgotten. After weeks of debating with one another about the distinction between cultural appropriation and cultural appreciation, students in my introductory course on black literature were convinced that something radical was happening, that these issues were "coming out in the open." Within a context where desire for contact with those who are different or deemed Other is not considered bad, politically incorrect, or wrong-minded, we can begin to conceptualize and identify ways that desire informs our political choices and affiliations. Acknowledging ways the desire for pleasure, and that includes erotic longings, informs our politics, our understanding of difference, we may know better how desire disrupts, subverts, and makes resistance possible. We cannot, however, accept these new images uncritically.

Eating the Other: Desire and Resistance

Dead: Carved Into Roses
from *Empire of the Senseless*

KATHY ACKER

A revolution has happened in Paris. Now the city lies in the hands of Algerians.
   Finally.
   More than two-thirds of the city has burnt down.
   A young mercenary, Abhor, is walking by the brown worm of a river. She
looks at the Seine and sees a rowboat, a boat that's falling apart, and in it, an old
dead man. She believes that this man is her father.
   And so the girl utters the following lament for her father and for the world of
her father, of white patriarchy:

The long-postponed realization of my dream conceived in the confines of
the cursed, obliterated city: hitching myself to the yoke, joining the horde
of Dervish camp followers and ex-whores trailing along in the wake of the
North African, mainly Moroccan, infantrywomen and soldiers of the Legion,
throwing away my useless high-heel shoes, sinking my bare feet into the
delicate ripples of the sands of what once must have been a city, Paris; lifted
lifted, thick sand dunes, walking on and on, losing myself in the desert.

   As if dreams were coming true, my dream finally: passing by the
Restaurant de l'Union, the mataam el-Jurria, the derb Sebbahi; with footsteps as supple and stealthy as those of a lover whom you believe you trust
and who's actually secretly poisoning you, for what reason?, as if you are
still nineteen years old and horny as hell, as if. This is your fortune, girl: A
refuge has lent itself to a thousand and one love duels. Each love was a tale
because a tail. Strong bodies have excited and refused you. This will
happen again. Everything will happen again.

   Within some drowsy Portuguese city whose streets and intersections are deserted in the full heat of the sun, you will meet a sailor. His dong itself will be a rebel against its tremendous nodding weight.

As far as sailing goes...

As for the victims of the negligence boredom and addictions of the owners, the French and the English owners, who've come down in this world; as for those former owners...

All humans and animals now sail over the same seas...

You're here now. At last. I've been waiting for you for what seems like a really long time. For a second. For a minute. For an hour. For a day. For a month. For a year. I knew you were going to come back to me. To the exact spot where we first met. In a river. In my cunt. I'm sopping wet. Let's fuck on top of this fountain. Splashing the waters of hydrochloric acid into my nostrils. Daddy. Pull off my fingernails. My back has been carved into roses. You scream that it's not only by you. As if you're alive or as if I'm not dreaming. As if I really possessed you and you really possessed me, we tore off each other's head and ate out the contents, then pecked out the remaining eyes, pulled out the sharks' teeth and sucked opium out of the gums, my vagina was bleeding. And I said to my father, the sailor, 'Let's not be possessed.'

Dead: Carved Into Roses

But like the rain, blood will always continue. Finally it didn't matter, in that driving rain, that everyone was staring at us. Finally it didn't matter that my squawks and our screeches of blood made the lunatics high up behind their asylum-barred windows mad. I alive and you dead together'll warm the bones of tombs. We together set splinters under their, the owners', fingernails, then light them up. We together made their dead bodies shrouded in soil into our beds. Only because they're dead, they envied our love which has been agony. We'll make the whole graveyard our playground because we're playing with ourselves. Then there'll be nowhere left to set on fire.

Soon there was nowhere left to set on fire. We wanted to travel, like sailors, but we had one living body and one dead body. The graveyard perished when you were buried in it. End. But what did I have left? Is a former victim an owner or no thing? From death, the place of your death you said that I, your daughter, would be nothing. But now my mind and the inside tips of my fingers and my lips and my mouth are blood.

Here I am, daddy my love, waiting for you to come.

When I woke up out of this insane dream, I realized that daddy's dead body, daddy was lying in some lousy Algerian hospital. Or that some dead old man's body was lying in some hospital for the dead. Stinking flies were probably eating it up.

'Why'd he kill himself?' Thivai asked. Thivai looked dead himself.

'Why's anyone kill herself?' Free of my dream, I shrugged. 'I don't know.'

'If anyone knows, you know.'

I examined my own blood: 'He had been trying to kill himself for a long time. It had taken him a long time. Because he was a tedious old fuck. Christ.'

Since he was now a tedious dead fuck, the new Algerian doctors were keeping him in a repulsive hospital in order to conduct experiments. Thivai and I knew that if they kept him in that hospital long enough, he'd die.

I had to get daddy out of the hospital.

Biker mags had informed me that prison and medical prisoners can escape their prisons only by faking death. In a manner such as this: Prison authorities usually bury the prisoners who they've tormented to death in mine shafts. In order to make sure each corpse is a corpse, they beat in each corpse's skull. But usually instead of beating in the corpses, they fuck the corpses and leave. It's no good beating about the bush. Most of the prisoners, after they've been beaten and tormented, prefer giving head to being dead. The now-homosexual prisoner, who's still alive, escapes.

Kathy Acker

If daddy became dead, I wouldn't be able to give him head anymore. I had to rescue him out of the evil hospital by making him go through his own death. I told Thivai all this.

'All I wanna know is who's gonna do the rescuing,' was what Thivai replied. He was cynical right down to the junk in his bones.

'Whoever gives the best head.'

Thivai, attractive like a junky, got the medical student who was in charge of wheeling corpses, for purposes of hospital household decoration, to fall in love with him. The young boy wheeled a corpse straight out of a window. The corpse was daddy. Night. Daddy fell right into my arms.

I was crying. In the nightmare of my mind, I desperately clung to that body as if it was alive. Like a shipwrecked sailor, I desperately clung to life. Thivai was no better, junked to the gills. But still human, not fish enough to swim through the depths of dreams. Sailors have huge dicks. Sailors have no hair and big arms.

But reality is something else. Reality is enough to make you crazy. For the loss of my dear love, I scream.

His rotting body lay on the concrete. Cut away. Slouching over bent almost double over a stinking hole enduring this brutal mistreatment stench flies blind you brush them away with useless arms. There was nothing left to do. So Thivai and I went and got tattooed. Carved into roses.

from "Numb"
from *Frisk*

D ENNIS C OOPER

Dear Julian,

Maybe you remember. In the early to mid-seventies we used to fuck and hang out for a few years, then you moved to Paris. Years later I ran into you at a club called The Open Grave in New York when I'd renamed myself Spit. We wound up fucking in your hotel. For the record, my first name is Dennis again. Spit was a really brief thing. He existed for maybe a year at most. I'm writing because I suspect you're the one human being I've ever known who'll understand what I'm trying to say, since I feel like I learned virtually everything when we were lovers. I know I seemed weird in that Spit phase, sorry. I'm writing in part to let you know how important you were and still are to me. I should have said so that night, but as you could tell by the pseudonym, I wasn't into connecting with people. I cut off everybody I loved or who loved me. I had to. I'm not sorry I did. I think you'll probably understand why if you just keep reading.

As you can tell by the stamp on the envelope, I live in Holland, Amsterdam to be exact. I originally came over here, meaning Europe, to find you. I spent a couple of weeks down in Paris. My address for you was two or three years out of date, but I eventually located your boyfriend who said you were vacationing in Morocco or something. I trained up to Amsterdam planning to kill time until you got back, but I ended up finding a place.

Anyway, the point is I'm writing to the Julian I imagine you to be. That's a guy who'll relate to the strange, ecstatic situation I'm in. Mainly I'm going to tell you some things because I'll flip if I don't. And I'm going to tell you my story chronologically, to keep myself clear. See how this sounds.

Okay, a year and a half ago I met someone in a coffee shop here where they sell marijuana and hash. They're both legal in Holland, as you probably know. He said he knew a place where I could live for a while. I felt so carefree or insane at that point I thought, Sure, why not live abroad. You'd done it. So this guy guided me to a man who was trying to rent out two floors in a windmill. Problem was the ground floor housed a small brewery, so the upper floors smelled like beer all the time. It's huge and incredibly cheap. Still, the smell's unbelievable, especially during the summer. All I own is a futon, a clock, and some cooking utensils. There's a stove, refrigerator. The floors are two large round rooms stacked on top of each other with a spiral staircase in the center and little porthole-shaped windows. The brewery keeps the rest of the building warm. My mom sends me cash every month via American Express, out of guilt for my fucked-up upbringing, I guess.

At first I just hung around clubs, bars, boy brothels (prostitution is legal), thinking I'd make friends or something. But Dutch guys are impossible, even the hustlers. They have these childishly beautiful faces that lead you to think they'll be open and sweet and so on, but it's a fluke because they're actually closed, repressed, insecure, arrogant people, all of which makes them more devastating to me, for some reason. I've never been hornier. For months I just walked around slackjawed and hard, since every second or third guy's perfection by my standards, but whenever I tried to begin conversations with them, they'd shut up and seem overly intellectual and chilled inside. Still, one year ago this extremely cute, sleepy-eyed guy about twenty-one came on to me at an after-hours club. He said I reminded him of an American ex-boyfriend. He was a ditsy, androgynous angel with brown hair, brown eyes, and big lips, just like every guy I've ever fallen for, including you. I forget his name. Call him Jan. When we got back here, Jan couldn't believe I actually lived in a windmill, the ultimate Dutch cliché. He found that hilarious. I toured him through the little brewery, which I'm allowed to keep an emergency key to. There's not much to see, just these four stinky tanks with open tops. After a while Jan said the smell was like sex, so we went back upstairs. He was tall, skinny, bigboned. He didn't smell very much, even inside his asshole. I've always been heavily into rimming. I got that from you, as you probably know. What's rimming about? I can't tell. I'm too obsessed. Anyway, I got wilder about Jan all during the sex, instead of more tired and bored like you're supposed to. It seemed really late. I think I was fucking him dog-style. He was stunning. I think he was moaning. I was about to come. I picked up an empty beer bottle without even thinking and hit the guy over the head. I don't know why. The thing broke. He fell off the futon. My cock slid out. He shit all over my legs and the bed on his way to the floor, which made me weirdly furious. I grabbed hold of his neck and ground the broken bottle into his

Dennis
Cooper

face, really twisting and shoving it in. Then I crawled across the room and sat cross-legged, watching him bleed to death. I stayed there all night, worn out, vaguely wondering why I didn't go phone the police, or feel guilt or sympathy for his friends. I guess I'd fantasized killing a boy for so long that all the truth did was fill in details. The feeling was already planned and decided for ten years at least. I've never felt less than amazed and relieved about the whole incident. Hours passed. At some point I dragged Jan upstairs to the top of the mill. There's a smallish room shaped like a bell that nobody's gone into for hundreds of years or whatever. I stuffed him inside and washed the stairs, floor. Whatever's left of the body is there. I've never checked. I'm not interested in a dead body's smell, no matter how cute it was. Nothing smells rotten down here, probably because of the brewery, like I said.

About three months later I killed a young boy who was hanging around outside the mill for some reason. He looked about fifteen, but he could have been anything up to twenty-one since the Dutch look like kids for a long time. Then, overnight, they turn into old hags. It's weird. I'd been smoking marijuana all day, so I was really relaxed. I found him standing in front of the door, looking up at the wheel, which doesn't revolve anymore and is locked into place. I asked if he spoke any English. He did, but not well. It was eightish p.m. Workers leave the brewery around five, so I asked if he wanted to see it. He said yeah. He was thin and stoop-shouldered with spiked black hair, like a lot of Dutch kids, wearing loose pastel-colored clothes, which is standard attire here. I showed him around, then I led him upstairs. He didn't say much or seem all that interested. We shared my last beer. He must have wanted to ask about what it's like in the United States, but he was too insecure about his English, I guess. I was starving for him. I can't remember why, except that he was particularly angelic. He must have noticed my hard-on. My pants were all bulged out, etc. I asked if he was a rich kid, which made him laugh. Then I asked if he needed some money. He looked at his shoes. I offered him five hundred guilders (about two hundred and fifty dollars) to take off his pants and let me lick his asshole. He snorted, still watching his shoes. I asked if he understood. He nodded. I said it wouldn't take long and he needn't get hard if he didn't feel up to it. He snorted again. I decided to just sit there staring at him. Eventually he muttered, five hundred guilders. His voice was high-pitched but very flat, like he was answering stupid questions all the time. I said, Sure. Then he shrugged. I asked him to strip. I stood a ways off to make him more comfortable. He took off everything but his undershirt, I don't know why. Would he rather lie down on his stomach or back? He said his back, and stretched out. I folded him into a ball, knees around his ears, weight on his shoulders, and told him to say if it hurt. When he answered,

from
"Numb"

Okay, I decided to kill him for some reason. Then I got so emotionally weird that I almost broke down. I licked his ass for a couple of minutes, half sobbing. He didn't notice. I do this thing where I wet down two fingers and slide them into an asshole then move them apart so the hole opens up all the way to the rectum. I lean over and sniff someone's bowels, I don't know why. This kid's was rank. I closed it up right away. He shut his eyes and let out regular breaths through his nose. I worked my hands under his shirt, which he didn't notice or mind. I played with his nipples. When that made him grin just the tiniest bit, I thought, Fuck it, why not, and grabbed his neck. He opened his eyes very wide. Otherwise he didn't fight me at all. It takes a lot longer to strangle someone than you'd think. At some point his eyes changed. They got kind of empty, fake. I noticed that diarrhea had squirted out of his ass, trickling all down his back. It smelled gruesome. When he was definitely a corpse, I ran over and leaned out a window. Occasionally I'd check to see if he'd moved. He hadn't. He looked so beautiful with his eyes empty, I don't know why. I walked back to the futon, sat down, and gazed into their glassiness a long, long time, daydreaming and numb. I didn't know what to do next, with his body I mean, so I kept it around for a few days pushed up against one of the walls. His skin got this weird dusky color. It was a very rough winter. Maybe that's why he didn't smell the whole time. I had a million ideas how I wanted to carve up and study the kid. I couldn't do it, I don't know why. Eventually I dragged him outside late one night and threw him into a canal that runs by the windmill, assuming somebody would find him and I'd be arrested. I don't know what actually happened because he was never reported either missing or dead in the papers or anything, as far as I can tell.

What's weird is he didn't fight back. He just accepted death. Every single time I've killed a Dutch boy this happens. It must be a part of the problem that makes them so cold and unknowable in general. They're like rabbits, at least in the sense that when a rabbit gets scared it freezes up. You can threaten to kick it, it won't move. If one of these boys ever actually fought with me now, I'd probably have a brain hemorrhage I'd be so shocked.

I just realized that if you're still reading you must be the person I want you to be. God, I hope so.

After the second time I got more methodical. That's been facilitated by these two German murderer guys. Jorg and Ferdinand live in a squat not far away from the mill. They're as fucked up as I am, just not as intelligent. They kill guys because it's a kick, whereas for me it's religious or something. I met them at a bar. Germans are more knowable than the Dutch. So I was talking drunkenly about the idea of murder to them and they told me they'd strangled somebody, a drunk, in Köln. That's why they'd moved

154

**Dennis
Cooper**

here to Holland, supposedly. They seemed really calm about things. When I was sure they were cool, I just casually mentioned the two boys I'd killed. They seemed amazed. They wanted to hear every detail. We officially joined forces that night, shook on it, all that. Since they basically don't give a shit who they kill just as long as it's gory, I get to handpick most of our victims and pretty much how the death happens. So I'm much more imaginative and violent now. They're big, muscly guys in their late twenties, but Ferdinand looks younger. Neither guy is particularly cute.

The weekend I met them we killed a guy who worked part-time at a fish market right near their squat. He was a typical Dutch yuppie guy who acted overly snotty whenever they came in to shop. They're kind of scruffy. Luckily for me he was almost my type. Except he was a dishwater blonde and had a very light mustache. Stores usually close at five p.m.; Tuesdays they're open till ten. He worked on Tuesdays with some older guy. Ferdinand, Jorg, and I drank at a bar up the street. Jorg has a fierce-looking pistol he carries around in his belt. When the fish market closed, the yuppie strolled up the street, past the bar, toward a bus stop. We followed him for a while. Then Jorg yelled, Let's do it. We ran. Jorg put the gun in the boy's back. It was weird, very crime movie. Ferdinand told him to shut up. He stiffened. We walked him rapidly toward the mill. An elderly couple walked by. I don't think we registered in their eyes. He didn't try to escape for some reason. As soon as we got him upstairs, Ferdinand and Jorg started punching and slapping him. They said it was "payback" for treating them shittily at the store. All he did was breathe hard and look frustrated. Jorg broke the yuppie's nose. At least it sounded that way. They kicked every part of his body. As a favor I stood around letting them get their frustrations out. Still, they fucked up the guy pretty bad. It wasn't uninteresting to watch, except I started to feel sympathetic toward him, which could be a problem someday. So I never let them go crazy again. He didn't fight or yell out, which was the most extreme case of the rabbit-syndrome thing I've ever seen. I don't know if it was pride or whatever. He was semi-unconscious when they quit the battering, etc. At my request, they dragged him onto the futon and cut off his clothes with a Swiss army knife, "accidentally" stabbing him lightly here and there. The guy's eyes were rolling around in his head. Once he was naked the Germans went over and stood by the fridge. They opened a couple of beers and started blabbing in German. The guy was all bruised and sliced up, but cute nevertheless, though I've seen better bodies. His legs were too hairy. So was the crack of his ass. The buttocks were saggy and thick. He had the faint beginnings of a beer belly. I rolled him onto his stomach and buried my face in his ass for a while. Jorg yelled, Hey Dennis, and threw me the knife. I stabbed the buttocks a couple of times. They didn't bleed. I rolled him over, pulled

from "Numb"

down my pants, and rubbed my ass on his face, which drove the Germans insane. They chanted, Shit, shit, shit. So I did, directly onto his mouth, stabbing his thighs every once in a while. Jorg ran over and stomped the shit into his face. I heard more stuff break in his head. I asked if they thought he was dead. Ferdinand asked if I wanted that. I said, Okay. Ferdinand picked up a kitchen knife, Jorg took the Swiss army knife, and they stabbed his chest, making "oof" noises. He bled really wildly. He had to be dead after that. I was standing there watching them, jerking off, when something weird happened that never reoccurred. Jorg came over, knelt down, and sucked my cock deep into his throat. I came in his head. I even thought I loved Jorg for the next day or two, though he acted like nothing had happened between us. Still, at that moment, for whatever reason, Jorg was starved for my sperm. Weird. Anyway, they grabbed the guy's body and dragged it downstairs, yelling how they knew a burial spot and they'd see me tomorrow. I spent all night cleaning the place. They buried the corpse by their squat, apparently. I thought that was risky. Still, we've never heard anything, so I guess it's okay.

Dennis Cooper

We've killed two other boys. The first was this punk, maybe twenty, twenty-one, whom I'd seen around town, always wearing the same filthy coat with the names of heavy metal bands scribbled all over it. Seeing him would make me ache for a couple of days, sometimes longer. Before I met Ferdinand and Jorg he seemed so impossible. But one afternoon I was walking around with the Germans when he came the opposite way, holding onto this one particular punk girl as always. I told the Germans I wanted to kill him. I'd learned how to say that without any feeling at all. Ferdinand said, That's no problem. It turned out the punk lived in their squat. They thought he was arrogant, stupid, pretentious, ugly, etc., so they were happy to help. They told me they'd just casually mention to him how they knew somebody who lived in a windmill. He'd definitely want a tour, they said. They'd try to coax him to visit that night. When we split off, I bought some rope so we could tie him if need be. They came by around eleven p.m. We opened beers, sat around. He listened more than he talked. I asked if he wanted a tour. He said, Okay. I showed him the tanks. At one point he strolled off alone, and I told Jorg and Ferdinand to wait for my signal. Ferdinand said I was obviously in love with the guy so no problem. The punk thought the brewery was cool. We went back upstairs, drank more beer. I was totally in awe. At one point I managed to ask, Are you gay? He said no but he didn't mind gays. I asked if he'd ever had sex with another guy. He said no, very blasé about it. I asked if he'd ever thought about fucking with gay men for money. He said yeah once. Ferdinand and Jorg sat there watching. I said, How about now with us? He laughed. Seriously? he asked. I said, Sure. He asked how much. I said, You tell us. He said, three hundred guilders plus two bags of heroin, which we had to score for him. I said, Fine. That kind of shocked him, I think. He leaned back and said, Oh, so that's what this bullshit's about. I said yeah. Then Jorg and Ferdinand left to score heroin. The boy said he had his own needle. We were alone, with him cross-legged facing me on the futon, acting like he knew he drove me totally insane. He asked a few questions, then nodded at the answers. I told him I'd wanted to fuck him for months, which made him look even more full of himself. I said, You've obviously done this before. He said yeah but we were lucky we'd asked when he was broke. The Germans came back with dope. He shot up. Then he stretched out on the floor by the fridge, very peaceful and pale, mumbling. I said, Let's move to the bed. He sort of staggered across the room, dropped face down on the futon. Stand him up, I said, Strip him. The Germans hoisted him up to his feet. First he said, Hey, what the fuck are you doing? Then he gave up and said, Oh okay. His clothes only looked complicated. They were a coat, T-shirt, pants, all of which slid right off. I said, Leave his boots on, I don't know why. His body was flawless—white, smooth, hard, dime nipples, big cock, dangly balls, square ass, hairless crack. He'd started nodding like junkies do. Hold him up, I said. I moved in close, feeling his body, especially his ass, which was so cold and soft. I told him I wanted to do everything that was humanly possible to him. He didn't say anything. He's too stoned, Jorg said. I asked Ferdinand, Will he fall if you guys let him go? They nodded. So let him go. They did. He collapsed on the floor and started groaning, but I don't think he was actually hurt. I stripped, knelt down next to his face and put my cock against his lips. I said, Suck. He opened his mouth. I started fucking it. That looked fantastic. At one point I stopped and French-kissed him, telling him how much I worshipped him. He was rubbing my back or my head while I did this. I licked down his body, tried sucking his cock. It wouldn't get hard, which made me furious for some reason. I don't know what I expected. I climbed off and told Jorg to kick the guy once in the stomach. He did. The guy balled up, retching. I told Jorg to hand me his gun. I pointed it at the guy's forehead. Open your eyes, I said, I'm going to kill you. He mumbled, No, no, no. The Germans came over and tied his wrists, ankles. Ferdinand said we should put something into his mouth. I thought he was saying my cock so I buried it. He probably meant a gag, but it's soundproof in here as far as anyone can tell. After a while Jorg suggested we carry the boy to the basically unused third floor of the mill and dangle him from the rafters. That way we could easily fuck him around, three on one. Great idea. The Germans started untying his ankles. I watched, jerking off. He was murmuring something in Dutch. They were ready to walk him upstairs, but I told them to hold it, I wanted to eat out his ass while his body was flexible. So

from
"Numb"

they laid him back down on the futon and contorted his hips until the asshole was totally accessible. They skinned back the cheeks with their fingers until it was a purple cave. I started nibbling and sucking it. I tried to blow it up like a balloon, pried it even more open, sniffed the depths, etc. The Germans thought that was ridiculous, as usual. I felt kind of lost and irrational. I'd never wanted to eat someone's shit before, but I was starved for the punk's. I asked him if it had been eaten before. He mumbled, No, let me go. I asked if he'd like me to eat it. He said, Are you really going to kill me? I said, No, very casually. Then I repeated my question. He said he didn't know what I meant. I said if he'd shit in my mouth we'd let him go. He said okay. He sounded totally exhausted. His ass looked fantastic. I stared at the thing for a few seconds. Then I put my hand under the hole. The punk looked terrified but kind of haughty. I think Dutch faces must have some haughtiness built into them or whatever. His neck was all crumpled up under his chin like a walrus's. I said, Shit. He contorted his face. A long shit squirted out. I had to move my hand around quickly to catch it all. I was so wild for the guy's looks in general that the smell hardly registered, but the Germans backed off and hooted, so it probably stank really bad. I started eating it. The Germans watched me, fascinated, I think, but pretending to puke and etc. It tasted okay, kind of bland. I swallowed three mouthfuls, then wiped off the rest on the floor and licked his asshole clean, inside, out. Then I said, Ferdinand, Jorg, take the idiot upstairs. He couldn't believe it. They grabbed him. He yelled, No, no, no. After we got him upstairs, the Germans threw a rope over a beam in the rafters. They untied his hands and retied them clasped over his head. Then they connected the two ropes and hoisted him until his feet were a foot off the floor. I stood nearby, jerking off. His face was scrunched up in discomfort, at the strain on his arms or whatever. It seemed religious, I don't know why. It also reminded me of a punching bag, like boxers use. Anyway, I was tired, so I told the Germans, Let's go downstairs for a while. The downstairs smelled gruesome, so Ferdinand opened the windows. I cleaned up the shit. We drank a few beers. The smell went away or we got used to it. There was no noise at all from upstairs, as far as we could tell. I asked Ferdinand and Jorg what they'd do with the punk if they could. They said what I knew they'd say, Beat him to death. I understood how that would be great and everything, but it wasn't enough somehow, at least for me. So I told them to go home, sleep, and we'd meet up the next day and finish the boy off, once I'd had some time to decide. They said, Fine, left. I was too tense to sleep. So I went back upstairs late that night and just watched the punk hang there. At first he didn't notice me. Then he said, Let me go, I won't tell, etc. I said, No, his death was important to me. He couldn't possibly understand, I said. Even I didn't understand, really. He tried to discuss it

**Dennis
Cooper**

with me intellectually. I said it wasn't a rational thing, he might as well give up. Then I caressed him all over. It was like I was frisking him, only much more extensively. All he said the whole time was his back hurt, almost to himself. I examined it. I couldn't tell what was the problem. So I knelt down and licked out his ass again, finger-fucked it. The fingering made him scream, because it put too much stress on his muscles, I guess. When he screamed his mouth opened incredibly wide. Then I really wanted to kill him. The red mouth triggered the need, because it was a preview or something. I went downstairs, came back up with the kitchen knife. He whispered, No, no, no, when he saw it. I said, Everything is over. I don't know why I said those particular words, but they seemed to communicate what I was feeling. I asked, Did he know it was over? He said, Yes, very flatly. I told him he was the most extraordinary and beautiful boy I'd ever seen in my life and that killing him would be incredible and that he should understand how profound his death was and that I would remember his murder forever. He just looked at me. I couldn't read his expression. My hands were totally trembling, but I took the knife and aimed it at his chest about the point where his heart would have been. He looked down to see where I'd aimed, by reflex, I guess. I shoved the blade about five inches into his chest with both hands. His eyes closed. He bit his bottom lip. His head dropped back. Blood poured out around the knife, down his body. I pulled out the knife and made a light horizontal cut across his stomach, which dribbled more blood. I stretched out his penis and tried to saw it in two. I only got through a fraction of it, it was so tough. I knelt down behind him and licked his asshole but that seemed kind of pointless with him dead, so I stabbed his back a bunch of times, kissing and licking his neck as I did. Then I walked back downstairs, dressed, went out, and called the Germans, waking them up. They hurried over. They kicked the corpse around for a while. That created a pretty hilarious fireworks display of blood, with him swinging around like the clapper in an invisible bell. I wanted the Germans to cut off his head for some reason, so they severed the rope suspending him and turned the corpse on its stomach. They sawed through its neck—carving, hacking, abrading, etc. The head came free, which took a very long time. Then they kicked the headless torso around. We were all soaked with blood, not to mention a clear goo that came from some organ inside him. I felt unbelievably tired and sat down against one wall, watching them dance around. When none of us cared about the corpse anymore, the Germans picked it up by the armpits and started downstairs. It had basically run out of blood. It didn't leave much of a mess on the stairs, just some smears where its feet dragged. They left the head behind resting on one ear. It continued to hold this incredible allure, but in a weird way, obviously, since it didn't mean much anymore. Jorg came back up for it shortly.

from "Numb"

I stood at the top of the stairs and watched the punk's body go. I couldn't see the head because it was under Jorg's arm, I think. Supposedly they weighted the corpse down with pieces of concrete and dropped it into the canal. Then I stashed the hypodermic and heroin in the refrigerator. The rest is a blur. For some reason this death is the one that has weirded me out more than any other. It's not an emotional thing, more a sleepiness that wasn't there before he died. It went on for weeks afterward and is still kind of here. I kept thinking I saw the punk places, in the far edges of my eyes, and so on. I never saw the punk's girlfriend again. Maybe the Germans killed her when I wasn't around since I know that Ferdinand, at least, was attracted to her. I should ask them.

**Dennis
Cooper**

*   *   *

Now you know. Here's what I'm hoping—you're who I believe you are, which means I hope you're like me, because we used to be so much alike, right? Trust me. I want you to live here with me and participate in this discovery, like we used to do in our teens, but with this major transcendence or answer I've found in killing cute guys. The Germans have gone to Portugal or somewhere for a while. So it'd be you and me. We'll do it ourselves. It's totally easy. Nothing's happened to me. I feel strong, powerful, clear all the time. Nothing bothers me anymore. I'm telling you, Julian, this is some kind of ultimate truth. Come on, do it. Am I wrong about you? Write to me care of the American Express office in Amsterdam.

Dennis

DENNIS. DON'T DO ANYTHING UNTIL I GET THERE. ARRIVING BY TRAIN 8 PM FRIDAY. BRINGING KEVIN WHO'S STAYING WITH ME. MEET US. JULIAN.

The Daddy Closet
from *On Our Backs*

MARCY SHEINER

When "Daddy's Little Girl" showed up in the offices of *On Our Backs,* it created quite a stir—several of us nearly fainted from intense levels of sexual heat. Since I recently had a story on the very theme of the Daddy fantasy rejected on legal grounds by a mainstream porno magazine, I questioned whether or not we could publish it. What ensued was a lively confessional dialogue about our own personal Daddy fantasies, punctuated by girlish giggles.

Most women who have Daddy fantasies say they are not envisioning their actual father, but rather the *gestalt* of Daddy: an authority figure, not necessarily a man, who doles out punishment but also protects and nurtures. Likewise, we don't necessarily see ourselves as children when in the scene, but as powerless sex objects wholly at the mercy of someone stronger than ourselves, just as in any scene involving dominance and submission. In the Daddy fantasy, chronological age is irrelevant—a mentality comes into play that appears to be ageless.

Nonetheless, there's no denying that negative reactions to sexual depictions of fathers and daughters, even if clearly spelled out as fantasy—as in "Daddy's Little Girl"—are based on valid concerns.

It goes without saying that incest and child abuse are always wrong. Sex between an adult and child can never be deemed consensual. Because of this, we're apt to experience guilt for having these fantasies, or for being turned on when we read a story like "Daddy's Little Girl." We repress or deny our feelings, leading to more guilt and confusion. But just as rape fantasies are not about actual rape, so too Daddy fantasies are not about actual incest.

Years ago I experimented with the Daddy fantasy in a literal sense, conjuring up an image of my father during masturbation, hoping to throw a light into that dark corner and illuminate a part of my psyche. I recalled being spanked as a child, and in a flash I remembered that every time my father's big masculine hand came down across my ass, it produced a corresponding pressure where my clitoris touched his knee.

The words that came to my mind as I masturbated were, "Please don't stop, Daddy, don't stop hitting me." When I came, I was laughing and crying simultaneously, as the utter innocence of the whole dynamic came crashing down upon my feminist consciousness. It had become crystal clear to me that whenever my father had turned me over his knee—relatively infrequently—I had most certainly enjoyed it simply because of the logistics: my clit was forced up against a hard object, his knee, and was subsequently stimulated. I was fairly awestruck by this revelation, since for years I'd assumed that my penchant for being spanked originated in self-loathing or masochism. It amazed me how such a simple dynamic could become so distorted over the years, each new attempt at analysis only adding another layer of shame to the original experience.

Spurred on by the success of this experiment, I extended my fantasies to visualizing my father during fucking. As it turned out, the incest taboo was stronger than my quest for self-knowledge, and my fascination for the fantasy was short-lived.

The shame and secrecy that permeate this topic is intense. It is not easy, for instance, for me to confess my thoughts on the subject, much less my fantasies. In fact, I'm downright terrified as I anticipate these words appearing in print beneath my name, revealing me to be an incestuous pervert. But I learned a long time ago that examination of sexual fantasies can help dissolve the guilt surrounding our sexuality, and can be as beneficial as years of psychotherapy or meditation.

Given the frightening overtones of the Daddy fantasy, then, it is understandably easier for most people to explore its power when the actual people are removed; that is precisely why genderbending—two women, for instance, playing out the fantasy—feels safer and is more likely to produce insights, not to mention orgasms.

There are many complex and even contradictory aspects to the roots of the Daddy fantasy. Probably the strongest element is the desire for a sexual partner who will love and nurture us no matter what. There's a telling scene in the film *The Misfits* in which Marilyn Monroe, tears streaming from her heavy hooded eyes, sobs to Clark Gable that he must have stopped liking her because he has expressed displeasure with her behavior.

"Come on, honey," he says, pulling her into his big bear arms, "didn't your Papa ever spank you, then pick you up and give you a big kiss? He did, didn't he?"

162

Marcy Sheiner

"He was never there long enough," sobs Marilyn. "Strangers spanked me for keeps." She collapses into Gable's arms: the quintessential little girl and the archetypal Daddy. (Unfortunately, the camera doesn't follow them into the bedroom, but my imagination has furnished the scene—and orgasm—quite adequately.)

As implied by this dialogue, there's a lesson conveyed to a little girl when her father spanks her for being naughty, then immediately showers her with affection. This is not to make a case for corporal punishment, but only to say that many of us were spanked as children and came to associate the act with love and/or sexual arousal. We may also have learned that punishment doesn't necessarily mean rejection—on the contrary, as Monroe's response implies, the absence of any kind of fatherly attention can be much more devastating than a slap on the rear. And though it's true that abused children often grow up to become abused women, in this case Monroe missed a vital experience, one that might have led her to tell those strangers who spanked her "for keeps" to fuck off.

The dynamics between Gable and Monroe are fascinating: she is at once a vulnerable little girl and a powerfully erotic adult woman. When she yields to him, she temporarily gives up her power, something Monroe frequently did with her leading men. Similarly, one friend I spoke to confessed that when she plays at having sex with a Daddy, she feels that she is relinquishing her coveted female powers to the force of "his" masculine desires. This is true whether or not the Daddy in question is biologically male or not—the same dynamics, she says, apply to butch/femme encounters.

Regardless of whether our daddies spanked and then kissed us as children, the yearning for an omnipotent lover who will stick with us through the pain is a powerful image that lies at the heart of most dominant/submissive fantasies.

When the word *Daddy* is introduced into this context, it carries a weight of added elements, even if we don't imagine our actual fathers. After all, how would it be possible for any intelligent woman brought up in the age of psychotherapy to not at least fleetingly wonder about the relationship between her sexuality and her father? We are repeatedly told that he carries a heavy influence over our self-development, that we seek out partners who remind us of him. How could it not occur to us that our relationship to him might carry elements of eroticism? Whether consciously acknowledged or not, a sexual scene involving a Daddy figure is fraught with Freudian overtones, the act shrouded in secrecy and the breaking of taboos. What could be hotter?

Another element that comes into play here is that we revert to the safety of infancy. Some psychoanalysts have postulated that, for heterosexual women, sucking a penis is the closest they ever come as an adult to

The Daddy Closet

sucking a breast. Slobbering over "Daddy's cock" can often put us in an emotional space akin to infancy; a time when we had no responsibility and did not know rules existed, much less what they might be. We simply responded to external stimuli, hopefully—but not always—of a nurturing quality. Significantly, it is almost always the word *Daddy*, not *father*, that carries so much erotic weight.

In fact, it is not only women who use the concept of Daddy for an erotic charge: witness the vast number of personal ads in gay men's magazines seeking father/son sexual relationships. Even more astounding is the fact that a significant number of heterosexual men with absolutely no homosexual experience harbor similar desires. In my work as a phone sex operator, my absolutely hottest calls involve reducing husky-voiced males to simpering infants through my impersonation of a cruel/loving big-dicked papa. It's profoundly moving to hear a grown man plead with me to "suck your big dick, Daddy," when I pretend I'm whipping it across his face, and then break down when I croon, "Come for Daddy, baby girl."

The bottom line is that, as in other dominant/submissive scenes, we're being coerced to engage in sex, thereby relieving us of guilt. When Daddy is the one doing the coercion, it goes even deeper; a parental figure is not only allowing us to be sexual, but also acknowledging us as sexual beings. We may have been given the message that sexual feelings are wrong, but if Daddy's making us do it, then it must be right. Furthermore, if we please Daddy sexually, we are rewarded by being thought of as or called a "good girl." A good girl, after all, is one who pleases her Daddy. The paradox is that in the Daddy fantasy we are also bad girls who incur Daddy's wrath and get punished. Thus, we get to be good and bad girls simultaneously—both highly erotic roles. We get to please Daddy, we get to be punished by her (or him), and in the end we're still loved. The ultimate jackpot is that Daddy forgives us for everything.

The question naturally arises as to why Mommy is so rarely conjured up to serve the same purpose, particularly among lesbians. The answer would appear to be the lack of erotic power Mommies have in our culture. Female sexuality in general is downplayed, and in the case of mothers, it's nearly eradicated.

Finally, it should not be necessary to state, but in these censor-filled times it apparently is (witness the rejection of my story), that articulating fantasies about Daddy is in no way an endorsement of child abuse. In fact, it's refreshing to find a story like "Daddy's Little Girl," in which someone is courageous enough to state the forbidden, implicitly giving the rest of us permission to speak the truth.

164

Marcy Sheiner

Daddy's Little Girl
from *On Our Backs*

ANN WERTHEIM

My Daddy comes into my bedroom late at night. She puts her hand under the blanket and up my nightgown and pushes her finger roughly up my pussy hole and whispers, "Daddy wants to fuck her little girl. Shh, you're wet already, you need this, don't you, that's a girl, good girl, Daddy is going to fuck her little pussy girl with her hard cock. That's what you want, isn't it?"

I traveled one hundred and fifty miles to play with this woman. We set it up for months, talked about it every which way. Her body pins me to the bed. I'm sleepy but aroused. "Yes, Daddy, please fuck me hard, please Daddy. I want your cock inside me."

I push my tongue into her ear, but she pulls away. "I'm going to give you a spanking in the morning, you know that don't you? In the morning at the breakfast table, I'm going to pull down your pants and give you a good, hard spanking. Might even have to use a belt on you, young lady."

"I'll be a good girl, Daddy, I promise."

"I know you will be, but you'll still get spanked anyway. Now take off your nightgown. Okay, hands up, spread your legs, that's my slut, Daddy's little slut, you just want that cock, don't you? Go on, beg for it."

"Your cock is so big, Daddy, it fills me up, I want you inside me, Daddy, please put your cock inside my wet pussy hole, please, Daddy, I spread my legs for you, my hole is always ready for your hard thick cock, I want it so bad, it's all I ever want. I think about your cock all day, Daddy."

"You better, you cunt. I'll teach you how to take care of Daddy's cock. You'll be the best little cocksucker around. Can you feel the head of my cock up against your pussy? Come on, reach for it, show Daddy you want it, that's a girl."

"Fuck me, Daddy."

But she doesn't fuck me yet. She grabs my hair and pulls/drags me onto the floor, and I'm crawling trying to keep up with her as she crosses the room to the full-length mirror. I'm confronted with the mirror image and try to look away, but she yanks my head back and says, "You're going to suck this cock, girl, and you're going to suck it good or I'm going to give you a beating like you've never felt before and wouldn't ever want to feel again—got that?"

"Yes, Sir."

And there we are in the mirror. For a second reality intrudes. I look up at her eyes, hidden by the brim of her cap, and her short white-blond hair. I've never seen her before and that increases my fear. On the phone it was like a confession to a priest, kneeling in the dark booth recounting my sins. I requested my own punishment in my search for forgiveness. And she doled out the punishment over the phone.

Ann Wertheim

I wrote line after line for her—one hundred lines, two hundred lines. I beat myself for her, for me, for Our Father—just another variation on a theme. But it was never enough. I never felt cleansed or redeemed or free. Finally she ordered me to come to her.

Now I'm on my knees, hands behind my back, and she's thrusting this big black dildo-cock into my mouth with one hand behind my head, and in her other hand she has the riding crop. Every time I slow down or gag she hits me hard with the crop. I cower and try my best to please her. My cunt is so wet I can feel the juice dripping down my leg. I want her to fuck me so bad. It feels like she could put a fist inside me, but all I can really think about is sucking her cock, trying to push it against her clit.

"That's a girl. Suck that cock. All my friends are watching you. You're making them hard, some of them are even rubbing themselves, they want to fuck this wet little mouth hole of yours. Show them how well you've been trained, you little slut. You'd suck all their cocks if I let you, wouldn't you? I'm going to let them cum all over you and make you lick it up. When I cum inside you, they'll cum all over your face."

I can actually feel all these people watching me—and then she makes me tell them a punishment story.

"Come on little girl, that's right, spread your cheeks, we all want to see that tight little hole of yours. And tell us what happens when you are a bad little girl."

"Daddy punishes me."

"And where do you get punished?"

"On my asshole. Daddy has a special stick and I have to hold my cheeks apart and count the strokes. After the stick, I usually get five strokes with the rubber dog whip."

Sometimes as punishment Daddy sticks her finger up my ass. At first it hurts, and then it feels good, but right about the time it feels good Daddy pulls her finger out really fast. She's says it is part of my training and eventually she'll fuck me up the ass with the dildo. She loves to look at my asshole, examine it: poke, prod, and lick my tight little hole. I feel a mixture of pleasure and humiliation. The humiliation usually wins out, especially if her friends are watching. She knows it too—you can hear it in her voice.

"What happens after your punishment?"

"I have special insertion training each night. A dildo is stuck up my pussy and then Daddy pushes one or two fingers into my asshole and teaches me to relax."

"I think it is very effective to punish girls in sensitive areas—minimum effort and dramatic effect. I'd say her behavior has improved considerably. Why don't you tell my friends where else you get your discipline?"

"On my clit."

"And?"

"On my breasts."

She puts on a latex glove and pushes three fingers up inside my cunt and pulls them out and slams in deep, so hard it hurts. Then I feel four fingers pushing up to her knuckles and I'm wet, but not that wet. "No, don't fist me. I can't take it, it hurts."

She says, "I want to teach you this, open up for me, do it for Daddy. We're going to work through this together. It'll hurt, but we'll handle this pain. I want you to do this for me."

I could feel her skin against my back, her small tits, hard nipples, her leather chaps touching my legs.

"Breathe deep and slow, breathe with me, that's it, feel the pain, through it, don't fight it, let the pain flow through you as you breathe. Stay with me, I want you to do this, it's important to me."

And then she's inside of me, her whole fist. It feels so good. She starts to pull out her fist and I don't want to let go. I clench my muscles down, she grabs my hair, cuffs my ears. She slaps me across the face.

"I'll teach you." Slap.

And I start to cry, not because it hurts, but because being slapped gets to me more than anything else. It is so intimate; it's my face. I'm scared and caught up in the fantasy, and she's still fucking me hard, wild and I want to touch her so bad, claw her, and I start pushing against her with my body.

She leaps off me, flips me over and starts hitting me with her belt, hard. My back, shoulders, ass, thighs. I try to get away, but I can't. She holds me down with one hand and flogs me with the belt, and I finally give in and start to scream and cry and sob. There are tears mixed with snot dripping down my face and I stop struggling. She puts down the belt, turns me over, enters me gently with her fingers and brushes the hair away from my face. We're close now, she's inside me, rocking rhythmically she kisses me, kisses the tears away, lots of kisses and licks.

"Shh, that's a good girl. Daddy loves her little girl, it's okay now, it's all over, it's okay, baby. You're so pretty, so wonderful, smart, sweet, you're a honey-bear, girl child. I'm here. I'm here. I'll take care of you."

"I'm sorry, Daddy."

"Sorry? You have nothing to be sorry about, it's okay, sometimes you have to fight and I'll have to beat you, but that's okay, that's what you need, and it's what I want and you're safe, sweetheart."

"I want my Daddy."

"I'm right here little girl. I got you and I won't ever let you go. It's okay, go to sleep now. You want some warm milk? Everything is going to be okay."

"Yes, Daddy. I love you Daddy." I curl up and sleep, secure that there will always be more punishments, but for now all is forgiven.

**Ann
Wertheim**

Epilogue: On Writing Pornography from *I Once Had a Master*

JOHN PRESTON

Many people ask how I began writing sexual fiction, how I go about doing it, and to what extent it's autobiographical. They ask in a way that's both shy and sly: shy because these people are talking about sex and sly because they seem to think they've "caught" me writing about it.

However much they reveal their intrigue about pornography and its creation, they almost always try to draw back the veil across their own faces. They attempt to deny any serious interest; most often that's done with a quick dismissive statement to me: "When are you going to do some real writing?"

I usually find these responses amusing; they're only occasionally even annoying. What *will* exasperate me are those literary people who express surprise that I "still" write pornography. These are usually those who think erotic fiction is a stage one might have to go through—probably for financial reasons—rather than any kind of goal a writer might ever aspire to. They seem to think that anyone who writes political essays, news journalism and even nonsexual novels shouldn't be involved in this kind of thing any more.

They certainly seem to think that the least I should do is move from their concept of "pornography" towards something they would label "erotica." I find the creation of this dichotomy between types of sexual fiction to be silly, as if these critics would like to cover the smell of bodily fluids with a goodly dose of perfume. I personally don't like to have sex with perfumed men so my descriptions will have to stay where my narration pays attention to physical odors.

Yet I have to admit that I had my own prejudices about pornography before I began to write it five years ago. In fact it was those preconceptions that allowed me to write it in the first place. But once I started writing sexual fiction I learned many things quickly. They all combined to alter how I envisioned sexual fiction—not just what I was writing, but what I read.

*   *   *

Writing isn't an easy occupation, certainly not in the beginning. It often appears to be, and I certainly thought it should be. I caught myself again and again saying, "I could do that." Thing was, I couldn't. Whenever I'd sit down and attempt to write, especially fiction, I would be instantly paralyzed.

The problems were self-inflicted. For one thing I thought anything that came out of my typewriter should be of high literary quality on the first draft; anything less was unacceptable, and that meant everything I did was unacceptable.

John Preston

But writing for gay magazines lifted some of these burdens, or so it seemed at first. It would only be writing about sex, I thought; it would only be pornography. If I chose I could hide behind a pseudonym. With little more thought than that I began. It might have been that I would only have done a story or two if *Drummer* hadn't been my first publishing contact.

Usually the editors of gay magazines have no time for editing in any real sense of the word. It's not a question of callousness on their part, nor necessarily of indifference. They are simply understaffed. The most response a writer can hope for is a request for a rewrite if something shows a lot of promise. *Drummer* can be quite different. Its editor—John Rowberry for most of the time I have published there—and its publisher John Embry have a more directive sense of their magazine and what should be in it.

My first submission was a short story which they thought worked well enough that they asked me to use it as the first chapter for a novel. If I would write it, they would serialize it. That first short story became *Mr. Benson,* now a book, and it altered what I could do in many ways.

But while *Mr. Benson* was being written, there were numerous other articles and stories that *Drummer* wanted. Their interest in me was heightened because I was then living in New York and could fill their need for more national editorial content than they were able to produce solely from their San Francisco base.

What this essentially meant was that I could avoid one of the most discouraging things a writer has to go through: finding someone interested in publishing his or her work. The results were mixed, but the reception remained warm and I continued.

The first thing that happened was that I altered the way I was looking at the world. I was constantly striving to find something new to write about and my day-to-day existence was the best place for me to investigate. Everything became sexual; there was no situation where I couldn't ind the setting for one of these pieces *Drummer* wanted. I'd walk into a deli and look at it as a potential site for an orgy. Every man I met was a possible character for future use. No piece of clothing could be dismissed until it had been examined as a fetish for some plot.

Now, I was hardly a sexual innocent at this point. Far from it: like many other young men from working-class towns, I had used hustling the nearest big city Greyhound terminal as a way to come out. But for as much action as I may have taken part in, there had been little available that helped me think about sex.

I had gone on to become actively involved in gay liberation but—especially during the time I was significantly part of that movement—it didn't want to deal with sex directly. If anything, the movement was anti-sexual. Everyone was so worried that straights would see us as people consumed with a vast orgasmic drive that we always tried to deny that the possibility even existed.

I had even tried to cope with the sexual reality of the world by entering a graduate program in human sexuality. But since the context was a state university worried about funding from a conservative legislature, the program didn't progress any further, really, than the rest of society. True, it was a "scientific" context and therefore didn't cloak sex with layers of romance and relational obligation, but it didn't seem to really work to have academia as the vehicle for examining this strange phenomenon's power and position in our lives. Lectures and panel discussions, sociological studies and psychological evaluation didn't always clarify very much. The mysteries of sex remained intact, more often than not, and their power to create misery and celebration even further obscured.

These were very strange times for me.

But what I discovered by writing about sex for *Drummer* was exciting. I began to encounter my own blocks to my own sexuality and my own capability for sexual intimacy. Why had I denied certain potentials? What did I think would happen to me if I took another step, went to a certain place, experienced a new act? Writing fiction let me look at those situations.

I experience writing pornography in precisely the same way I expect people who read pornography do—as an examination of possibilities and potentials. Since I had freed myself from any literary restraints other than the telling of a good story, I could address myself to my own discoveries.

I think many of those stories had a glee about them. I know I had that sense of fun while doing the writing. I felt as though I were saying to a whole group of people, "Come and look at this one. You won't believe what I've done this time!"

Then three things happened in quick succession. My articles and sto-

**Epilogue:
On Writing
Pornography**

ries began to appear on the newsstand. (Most people don't realize that there's a lag of many months between writing and publication.) It is difficult to explain just how different it is to see one's words in printed form rather than typewritten on paper; the impact can be amazing. While I was facing this dilemma I also had to face another that was utterly unexpected: people not only read what I wrote, they wanted to talk about it, they wrote letters, they stopped me on the street. Finally, while I was still reeling from these stuns, *Mr. Benson's* serialization began.

I've never fully understood just why *Mr. Benson* became quite so popular. There were fan clubs, letter, and T-shirts. Some raw nerve had been struck. This was totally unanticipated. When I had finished the book, the publisher called one day and asked what name I wanted to use with it. I simply went along with his assumption that I should take a pseudonym. Why use my real name? No one was going to notice the author anyway. But in fact, they did. *Drummer,* and now other magazines, wanted more articles and more fiction from me. I had earned a new identity: pornographer.

I didn't duck this label. On the contrary, I wrote more and I began to photograph male nudes as well—a great enjoyment. I still thought I was only trying to tell a story, often one inspired by a specific photographic image or a particular erotic memory. But as the pages mounted, I couldn't help but see that there were certain themes which ran through most of what I did.

There was the sense of exploration that I've commented on. Also a perception of sex as a cathartic experience. Most of all, there was an implicit judgment that to avoid a sexual experience was to lose an opportunity for a whole range of personal investigations that went far beyond a genital experience. I realized that sex, for me, never happened in a vacuum: it was always something that could alter a person's perceptions of the world and even his position within it.

I also learned something important about myself as a writer. While I don't think I indulged in a self-deception of myself as a member of any literati, I realized that the responses I was getting from readers were making me take much of my writing more seriously.

The fact that I began my writing with *Drummer* had a great deal to do with this. More than any other gay magazine *Drummer* knows precisely to whom it's directed. There is a very specific audience and that audience cares tremendously about what's in the magazine's pages. There is a sense of unity about *Drummer* that few publications have; perhaps only a periodical like the *New Yorker* is comparable, for instance in the way advertising copy is as much an integral part of the final package as the fiction and editorial reportage.

John Preston

Because I had read *Drummer* for years before I wrote for it, and because I identified myself as one of its readers, I suppose I had an intrinsic sense of who the rest of the readers were, how they would see things, what they would like to hear and how to use what words to communicate what emotions to them.

I had begun by writing fiction that was heavily fantasy-laden. Certainly that's true with *Mr. Benson.* Increasingly I wrote things that people could see as possibilities for themselves. The fantasy became less and less important. Instead a constant return to looking at what really happened in gay life and what could be made out of it took over, emotionally and sexually. If I hadn't liked the people who read gay magazines and gay books in general, I might never have seen that pornography holds a rather unique place as a vernacular literature in the gay world, more so than elsewhere.

It was at about this time that I picked a guide for myself. Like most other people, I had used pornography in one way or another since I had begun to be sexual. As I realized that some people separated out my own work and that of some other writers such as T.R. Witomski and Dennis Schuetz, I remembered that certain work I had read had made a great impact on me, certainly greater than what I usually expected to receive from sexual writing.

I retraced my reading and discovered that most of the books and stories that had stood out so starkly from the rest of the erotic fiction I had known had been written by one person, Samuel Steward. This was the man who had published the Phil Andros novels, which are now having such a deserved rebirth in new publication. I went on to discover a lot more about him and his life and even made what I've always called a "little pilgrimage" to meet Steward in California.

Steward and his career helped me put myself and my work into a context. He certainly ripped away any shreds of self-deprecation I might have still had about being an erotic writer. His forays into sexual fiction hadn't defined him in any constraining manner and he—after all, he was a protégé of Gertrude Stein's—felt free to move back and forth between pornography and any other kind of writing he chose to do.

My investigation of Steward's work was no minor inquiry. I started work on a biography of him, a project short-circuited only by the publication of his own autobiography. Most of the lessons I learned from Steward were things I already had begun to have a grip on, but my awareness of them became more conscious, and the decision to use certain perceptions and to include certain kinds of information were given a more solid foundation because of his example.

I can define some specifics; for one thing, there is nothing wrong with writing something that is essentially meant to be just an entertainment.

**Epilogue:
On Writing
Pornography**

(There sometimes seems to be some prejudice that writing should be always *meaningful* and often difficult; this is not dissimilar to the view that medicine should taste bad, I suppose.) Sex is first and foremost fun. Sex is desired and desirable. If these rules are broken, it's a sure sign someone's being dishonest, misusing sex or someone else, or in some other way, somebody is mixing up the works. Still, it's always true that sex seldom happens alone; it produces emotions and it flows from emotions.

There's still another statement to be made that had great importance to Steward: writing about sex is one of the best ways possible to inform the gay world about itself, including issues with which it should be concerned and potential problems it might face.

When Steward and a few other gay writers began their publishing careers—in terms of *gay writing*—they were limited to sexual themes because their only hope for publication was sleazy pornographic publishing houses. Only by meeting the erotic requirements of those houses could a writer like Sam Steward inform his readers about disease and its spread, the danger of police entrapment, the locales of gay gathering places, and more.

There is still another level where Steward's point of view informed me about my own values. When we talked and wrote about our readers, it was very apparent that he also actively liked the gay men who would read our writing. At one level it might seem a minor point, but it became increasingly relevant to me. I learned to see when writers didn't like their readers; there is a certain voice in much writing that makes apparent its disdain for the reader. Whatever else it had no place in erotic fiction, at least not what we are writing. It would be a mean-spirited piece of fiction that invited someone to share a fantasy that was presented in such a way that the guest was unwelcome.

Numerous forces removed some of the focus of my sexual fiction for a while. They were mainly financial considerations which led me to write a whole body of work that was mercifully published pseudonymously and was most often directed at groups other than gay men. I have written erotic fiction for lesbians, straight men, and straight women. I have worked in what was essentially a porn factory, churning out a required number of pages per week. I have contracted to write entire magazines under a whole list of pen names. I did like some of this; I'm embarrassed by a lot of it; I hope you never discover parts of it.

When people talk about writing pornography as though it were some great ordeal for a writer, they are often referring to situations such as those I've just described, but those are not always as dark as they may seem. There is still the constant use of one's craft and the practice at writing that is invaluable, or can be. It's the sense of frustration at being trapped in

174

John Preston

such situations that bothers most writers, I think. Unless you are really judging sex and writing about sex with a special heaviness, it is no different than being stuck for a time writing for a hopelessly provincial newspaper while waiting for your skills to be sharpened well enough for you to take advantage of an opportunity to move on, either to a more exciting journal or to a more freewheeling freelance situation.

In any event, I was able to expand what I wrote. I didn't stop writing about sex—far from it—but I increasingly found other pleasure and income writing other types of fiction as well as nonfiction. But wherever I went, the initial experiences of writing pornography remained my foundation as a writer, that thing that gives me a place to stand: I like my readers; I care about their reactions and what is happening to them.

I think my journey has been different than most writers', though I'm hardly unique to have earned a living as a pornographer. Nor did that experience take me to a wholly different place than many other gay writers. Most of us end up in the same arena.

Taken as a group, gay writers do spend more time dealing with sexual issues than do others. There are reasons for it. Gay life treats sex differently. It can be a symbol for self-affirmation—and self-abuse—in a way that often just doesn't translate for other people. A gay man will understand the enormous potential symbolism of being fucked for the first time in a unique way, that it is not an act comparable to losing one's virginity. It can mean much more that that.

Most interestingly, sex is not the end result of an emotional relationship in the gay world, at least not often. That, of course, is the most common depiction of sex in heterosexual and lesbian fiction. Instead, sex is most often the harbinger of emotional relationship that may develop.

We see sex differently. We experience it differently. Often our sex partners are not the most important people in our lives at the moment, but they have the potential of becoming that and our elation when they do—or our response when they don't—informs us of our emotional make-up in a very visceral manner.

More: it is also true that the sex we have is precisely that which initially separates us from the rest of society in the most fundamental way. It is the first essential reason we are alien in this world and therefore it can't be ignored. Its impact is simply too great to be shunted aside.

One of the reasons we constantly return to sex is—I think—that we are always needing to know if this is enough to justify what we go through because of it. Often that's an emotional issue: are these emotions worth it? But because the repercussions are so enormous it becomes a political and social issue as well.

Sex is a part of our identity; it's how we relate to many of the most

Epilogue: On Writing Pornography

important people in our lives; it's the vehicle for our most intensely powerful relationships.

It doesn't follow that pornography always addresses all these issues as seriously as it might—not by any means. It could be the equivalent to a Polaroid snapshot of genitalia. Someone would get off on it and it may be sufficient that that photograph helped produce an orgasm to fit the definition. I have taken those photographs and I've written the parallel to them in some pornography. Nor does it follow that sexual writing must deal with all these issues in some intensely analytic fashion—though it might. It is perfectly adequate that it simply be an entertainment.

Sexual writing parallels all the possibilities with which we could deal with sexual activity. We can have sex that's as functional as the shooting of a Polaroid camera or as joyfully uninvolved as a Saturday matinee; we can use it to express our honest emotions or we can laden it with the luggage of our deepest needs.

John Preston

*   *   *

I find this an interesting progression I've undergone: from the beginning as a writer producing sexual work precisely because he hadn't cared about it, hadn't thought it would be taken seriously and therefore hadn't any need to worry about the quality of the writing and its reception, to the place where I can attempt to write sexual fiction of the greatest familiarity.

And it does parallel my existence as a gay man. I am far from that New England boy who hitched the backroads of Massachusetts hoping for an anonymous hand to rest on my thigh. Just as I would find no satisfaction today in taking a Polaroid photograph of a flaccid penis, so do I insist on more from other men and myself when we share our bodies with one another.

BOOKS FROM CLEIS PRESS

SEXUAL POLITICS

Forbidden Passages: Writings Banned in Canada introductions by Pat Califia and Janine Fuller.
ISBN: 1-57344-020-5 24.95 cloth;
ISBN: 1-57344-019-1 14.95 paper.

Good Sex: Real Stories from Real People, second edition, by Julia Hutton.
ISBN: 1-57344-001-9 29.95 cloth;
ISBN: 1-57344-000-0 14.95 paper.

The Good Vibrations Guide to Sex: How to Have Safe, Fun Sex in the '90s by Cathy Winks and Anne Semans.
ISBN: 0-939416-83-2 29.95 cloth;
ISBN: 0-939416-84-0 16.95 paper.

I Am My Own Woman: The Outlaw Life of Charlotte von Mahlsdorf translated by Jean Hollander.
ISBN: 1-57344-011-6 24.95 cloth;
ISBN: 1-57344-010-8 12.95 paper.

Madonnarama: Essays on Sex and Popular Culture edited by Lisa Frank and Paul Smith.
ISBN: 0-939416-72-7 24.95 cloth;
ISBN: 0-939416-71-9 9.95 paper.

Public Sex: The Culture of Radical Sex by Pat Califia.
ISBN: 0-939416-88-3 29.95 cloth;
ISBN: 0-939416-89-1 12.95 paper.

Sex Work: Writings by Women in the Sex Industry edited by Frédérique Delacoste and Priscilla Alexander.
ISBN: 0-939416-10-7 24.95 cloth;
ISBN: 0-939416-11-5 16.95 paper.

Susie Bright's Sexual Reality: A Virtual Sex World Reader by Susie Bright.
ISBN: 0-939416-58-1 24.95 cloth;
ISBN: 0-939416-59-X 9.95 paper.

Susie Bright's Sexwise by Susie Bright.
ISBN: 1-57344-003-5 24.95 cloth;
ISBN: 1-57344-002-7 10.95 paper.

Susie Sexpert's Lesbian Sex World by Susie Bright.
ISBN: 0-939416-34-4 24.95 cloth;
ISBN: 0-939416-35-2 9.95 paper.

FICTION

Another Love by Erzsébet Galgóczi.
ISBN: 0-939416-52-2 24.95 cloth;
ISBN: 0-939416-51-4 8.95 paper.

Cosmopolis: Urban Stories by Women edited by Ines Rieder.
ISBN: 0-939416-36-0 24.95 cloth;
ISBN: 0-939416-37-9 9.95 paper.

Dirty Weekend: A Novel of Revenge by Helen Zahavi.
ISBN: 0-939416-85-9 10.95 paper.

A Forbidden Passion by Cristina Peri Rossi.
ISBN: 0-939416-64-0 24.95 cloth;
ISBN: 0-939416-68-9 9.95 paper.

Half a Revolution: Contemporary Fiction by Russian Women edited and ranslated by Masha Gessen.
ISBN: 1-57344-007-8 $29.95 cloth;
ISBN: 1-57344-006-X $12.95 paper.

In the Garden of Dead Cars by Sybil Claiborne.
ISBN: 0-939416-65-4 24.95 cloth;
ISBN: 0-939416-66-2 9.95 paper.

Night Train To Mother by Ronit Lentin.
ISBN: 0-939416-29-8 24.95 cloth;
ISBN: 0-939416-28-X 9.95 paper.

Only Lawyers Dancing by Jan McKemmish.
ISBN: 0-939416-70-0 24.95 cloth;
ISBN: 0-939416-69-7 9.95 paper.

The Wall by Marlen Haushofer.
ISBN: 0-939416-53-0 24.95 cloth;
ISBN: 0-939416-54-9 paper.

We Came All The Way from Cuba So You Could Dress Like This?: Stories by Achy Obejas.
ISBN: 0-939416-92-1 24.95 cloth;
ISBN: 0-939416-93-X 10.95 paper.

LESBIAN STUDIES

Boomer: Railroad Memoirs
by Linda Niemann.
ISBN: 0-939416-55-7 12.95 paper.

The Case of the Good-For-Nothing Girlfriend by Mabel Maney.
ISBN: 0-939416-90-5 24.95 cloth;
ISBN: 0-939416-91-3 10.95 paper.

The Case of the Not-So-Nice Nurse
by Mabel Maney.
ISBN: 0-939416-75-1 24.95 cloth;
ISBN: 0-939416-76-X 9.95 paper.

Dagger: On Butch Women edited
by Roxxie, Lily Burana, Linnea Due.
ISBN: 0-939416-81-6 29.95 cloth;
ISBN: 0-939416-82-4 14.95 paper.

Dark Angels: Lesbian Vampire Stories
edited by Pam Keesey.
ISBN: 1-57344-015-9 24.95 cloth;
ISBN: 1-7344-014-0 10.95 paper.

Daughters of Darkness: Lesbian Vampire Stories edited by Pam Keesey.
ISBN: 0-939416-77-8 24.95 cloth;
ISBN: 0-939416-78-6 12.95 paper.

Different Daughters: A Book by Mothers of Lesbians edited by Louise Rafkin.
ISBN: 0-939416-12-3 21.95 cloth;
ISBN: 0-939416-13-1 9.95 paper.

Different Mothers: Sons & Daughters of Lesbians Talk About Their Lives
edited by Louise Rafkin.
ISBN: 0-939416-40-9 24.95 cloth;
ISBN: 0-939416-41-7 9.95 paper.

Dyke Strippers: Lesbian Cartoonists A to Z edited by Roz Warren.
ISBN: 1-57344-009-4 29.95 cloth;
ISBN: 1-57344-008-6 16.95 paper.

Girlfriend Number One: Lesbian Life in the 90s edited by Robin Stevens.
ISBN: 0-939416-79-4 29.95 cloth;
ISBN: 0-939416-8 12.95 paper.

Hothead Paisan: Homicidal Lesbian Terrorist by Diane DiMassa.
ISBN: 0-939416-73-5 14.95 paper.

A Lesbian Love Advisor by Celeste West.
ISBN: 0-939416-27-1 24.95 cloth;
ISBN: 0-939416-26-3 9.95 paper.

More Serious Pleasure: Lesbian Erotic Stories and Poetry edited by the Sheba Collective.
ISBN: 0-939416-48-4 24.95 cloth;
ISBN: 0-939416-47-6 9.95 paper.

Nancy Clue and the Hardly Boys in
A Ghost in the Closet by Mabel Maney.
ISBN: 1-57344-013-2 24.95 cloth;
ISBN: 1-57344-012-4 10.95 paper.

The Night Audrey's Vibrator Spoke: A Stonewall Riots Collection
by Andrea Natalie.
ISBN: 0-939416-64-6 8.95 paper.

Queer and Pleasant Danger: Writing Out My Life by Louise Rafkin.
ISBN: 0-939416-60-3 24.95 cloth;
ISBN: 0-939416-61-1 9.95 paper.

Revenge of Hothead Paisan: Homicidal Lesbian Terrorist by Diane DiMassa.
ISBN: 1-57344-016-7 16.95 paper.

Rubyfruit Mountain: A Stonewall Riots Collection by Andrea Natalie.
ISBN: 0-939416-74-3 9.95 paper.

Serious Pleasure: Lesbian Erotic Stories and Poetry
edited by the Sheba Collective.
ISBN: 0-939416-46-8 24.95 cloth;
ISBN: 0-939416-45-X 9.95 paper.

REFERENCE

Putting Out: The Essential Publishing Resource Guide For Gay and Lesbian Writers, third edition,
by Edisol W. Dotson.
ISBN: 0-939416-86-7 29.95 cloth;
ISBN: 0-939416-87-5 12.95 paper.

POLITICS OF HEALTH

The Absence of the Dead Is Their Way of Appearing
by Mary Winfrey Trautmann.
ISBN: 0-939416-04-2 8.95 paper.

Don't: A Woman's Word
by Elly Danica.
ISBN: 0-939416-23-9 21.95 cloth;
ISBN: 0-939416-22-0 8.95 paper

1 in 3: Women with Cancer Confront an Epidemic edited by Judith Brady.
ISBN: 0-939416-50-6 24.95 cloth;
ISBN: 0-939416-49-2 10.95 paper.

Voices in the Night: Women Speaking About Incest edited by Toni A. H. McNaron and Yarrow Morgan.
ISBN: 0-939416-02-6 9.95 paper.

With the Power of Each Breath:
A Disabled Women's Anthology
edited by Susan Browne, Debra Connors and Nanci Stern.
ISBN: 0-939416-09-3 24.95 cloth;
ISBN: 0-939416-06-9 10.95 paper.

Woman-Centered Pregnancy and Birth
by the Federation of Feminist Women's Health Centers.
ISBN: 0-939416-03-4 11.95 paper.

AUTOBIOGRAPHY, BIOGRAPHY, LETTERS

Peggy Deery: An Irish Family at War
by Nell McCafferty.
ISBN: 0-939416-38-7 24.95 cloth;
ISBN: 0-939416-39-5 9.95 paper.

The Shape of Red: Insider/Outsider Reflections by Ruth Hubbard and Margaret Randall.
ISBN: 0-939416-19-0 24.95 cloth;
ISBN: 0-939416-18-2 9.95 paper.

Women & Honor: Some Notes on Lying
by Adrienne Rich.
ISBN: 0-939416-44-1 3.95 paper.

LATIN AMERICA

Beyond the Border: A New Age in Latin American Women's Fiction
edited by Nora Erro-Peralta and Caridad Silva-Núñez.
ISBN: 0-939416-42-5 24.95 cloth;
ISBN: 0-939416-43-3 12.95 paper.

The Little School: Tales of Disappearance and Survival in Argentina
by Alicia Partnoy.
ISBN: 0-939416-08-5 21.95 cloth;
ISBN: 0-939416-07-7 9.95 paper.

Revenge of the Apple by Alicia Partnoy.
ISBN: 0-939416-62-X 24.95 cloth;
ISBN: 0-939416-63-8 8.95 paper.

You Can't Drown the Fire: Latin American Women Writing in Exile
edited by Alicia Partnoy.
ISBN: 0-939416-16-6 24.95 cloth;
ISBN: 0-939416-17-4 9.95 paper.

ORDERING INFORMATION

We welcome your order and will ship your books as quickly as possible. Individual orders must be prepaid (U.S. dollars only). Please add 15% shipping. Pennsylvania residents add 6% sales tax. Mail orders to:

Cleis Press
P.O. Box 8933
Pittsburgh PA 15221

MasterCard and Visa orders: include account number, expiration date, and signature. Fax your credit card order to (412) 937-1567, or telephone Monday– Friday, 9 am–5 pm EST at (412) 937-1555.